Praise for THE GREEN INTENTION

"The cutting edge of the environmental movement is the interface between outer and inner environment — the ways in which taking care of our planet and taking care of our souls go hand in hand. *The Green Intention* illuminates the deepest meaning of sustainable living, taking the conversation of how to create a healthier planet to a deeper and more sacred place."

MARIANNE WILLIAMSON

"*The Green Intention* is the only book that connects the inner sense of individual life-purpose with the outer intention of living green for the benefit of all beings and the planet. Every page is filled with the inspiration to "live green" from the inside out."

MICHAEL BERNARD BECKWITH
author of *Spiritual Liberation-Fulfilling Your Soul's Potential*

"For a sustainable future, we all need to think green. We need to think green spiritually which changes our mental, our physical, and the ecological world. You will love Sandy and Deanna's book."

MARK VICTOR HANSEN
co-author of *Chicken Soup for the Soul*

"*The Green Intention* is an amazing guide to living a harmonious life in spirit and in balance with Mother Nature. 'Sustainable Spirituality' for the mind, body, soul and the planet — this new genre of inspirational material will motivate you to change your life and the world."

RON & LISA BERES
authors of *Just Green It!*

The only ethical decision
is to take responsibility for our
own existence
and that of our children.
Make it now.
Cooperation, not competition,
is the very basis of existing life systems
and of future survival.
Though the problems of the world
are increasingly
complex, the solutions remain
embarrassingly simple.

BILL MOLLISON
Founder of Permaculture

The Green Intention

LIVING IN SUSTAINABLE JOY

SANDY MOORE *and* DEANNA MOORE

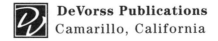 **DeVorss Publications**
Camarillo, California

ISBN: 9780875168555
FIRST EDITION, 2011

DeVorss & Company, Publisher
PO Box 1389
Camarillo CA 93011-1389
www.devorss.com

 Printed in the United States of America
This book is printed on recycled environmentally friendly paper.

—————————————————————————

Library of Congress Cataloging-in-Publication Data

Moore, Sandy
  The green intention : living in sustainable joy / Sandy Moore and Deanna
Moore. — 1st ed.
     p. cm.
  ISBN 978-0-87516-855-5 (trade pbk. : alk. paper) 1. Green movement.
  2. Environmental protection. I. Moore, Deanna, 1990- II. Title.
  GE195.M655 2010
  333.72—dc22
                                    2010035867

Table of Contents

ACKNOWLEDGEMENTS

My acknowledgements run deep and wide. I would like to begin by thanking the brilliant and magical editors who brought this book from idea to form. First, I am grateful to Robin Quinn who used her genius to mold my years of ideas into a beautiful teaching manuscript. Next, to my dear friend and soul sister, Shannon Ingram, who helped me to weave my heart and soul into the words that fill these pages. And to beautiful Marguerite Bonnett who shared her great gifts with me to bring it all together. Finally, to Diane Nixon, Kathy Jones and Kathy Juline whose editorial review and comments made a huge difference in completing the book.

I want to thank all of the beautiful souls whose lives have been "touched by Tara" and who came to our store, Tara's Angels. You are the inspiration behind my words and the encouragement to continue my journey.

Words cannot express my appreciation for Jackie and Matt Belzano and Diane and Armand Lofchie who have been like beloved parents and coaches to me over the years. My spiritual teachers deserve my heartfelt thanks – Jean Houston, Sai Maa Lakshmidevi, Brother Ishmael Tetteh, Rev. Dr. Michael Beckwith and the late Ernest Holmes have helped to form the essence of who I am today.

My treasured friends have truly enriched my life. Jenny LeBel is an angel who has often believed in me more than I have believed in myself; Michelle Spieker, another soul sister whose support, encouragement and guidance has been invaluable in so many ways; Terry and Marilyn Taylor, who have stood by my side through thick and thin, and paved the way for the unfolding.

My heart is filled with gratitude for my extended church family – all of you who have mirrored my love and support over the years. There are too many names to include, but each of you is very important to me and I love you.

I give thanks for my parents, George and Helen Souther. Mom gave me the legacy of a great sense of humor and Dad instilled in me the joy of keeping my mind awake and alert for continuous learning

I am profoundly grateful to my immediate family. I know it was no accident that we chose each other to share this life together. Thank you to Kirk, my best friend and confidant, soul mate and partner, husband and lover. Without you I don't know who I would be. You have been there with me through all of life's ups and downs—I love you. And thank you to my beautiful children, Deanna and Tara, who have been my greatest teachers. They are brilliant, courageous, funny and fun.

Most of all, I am grateful to God.

Sandy Moore

ACKNOWLEDGEMENTS

I have been blessed with many teachers in my life, human and non-human. A deep well of gratitude expands out from my soul and into all my family, friends, healers, teachers, children, species, plants and animals that I have come to know.

I give thanks for all of the beauty and all of the pain of the world. They are our teachers.

Thank you to Nature for your peace & inspiration and profound knowing. To the plant world, oak trees, redwood trees, cacao trees, coastal sage, deer tracks, foxes, sacred fires, crescent moons, rocks and sandstone cliffs at the edge of ocean. You are why I am here.

Thank you to my parents, Kirk and Sandy, for your vision, consciousness, communication, empowerment, fun, and unconditional love. You embrace me with acceptance and support, and encourage me to be my best. I am honored and blessed to be part of this journey with you.

Thank you to Jodi Levine for consistently believing in me. Layers deep of gratitude for your patience, timeless support, openness, kindness, and acceptance. You have been my balance, my teacher and my best friend. Thank you for your profound connection to the earth and commitment to the generations to come. You continue to inspire me beyond words. You are solid like a desert rock.

Thank you to Daniel Francis, who inspires me continually with intellectual food, emotional evolution and wise reflections. You make me laugh the most.

Thank you to Eric Humel for your love of seeds and commitment to taking me to the ocean to ride waves.

Thank you to Michelle Spieker, for being my mentor, my support for all of my projects, and an exquisite visionary. You are an amazing being and cherish our connection.

Thank you to all of my teachers: Chris Prelitz, Jean Houston, Lynne Twist, Jon Young and the countless others, for the reconnection.

And Thank you to my support in the Spirit World: Tara and Grandmother Grey and every being who supports me in the other dimensions of life.

Deanna Moore

Introduction

Heaven is under our feet, as well as over our heads.
HENRY DAVID THOREAU

I want to know how to narrow the gap between
the sincerest desires of my soul and my daily actions.
ORIAH MOUNTAIN DREAMER

Everybody is thinking green these days, whether out of concern for the planet or the pocketbook. I believe thoughts become things. Being green means caring deeply about yourself, your environment, your family, friends and associates and especially about your planet. Kermit the Frog said, "It's not easy being green." I beg to differ with the famous frog. It's easy being green when it means you are living your best life.

A student consciousness is extremely important throughout life — to continually be willing to learn and grow. Like most wide-eyed learners, I have had countless opportunities to shut down and stunt my growth. In 1992, while living a peaceful, happy life as a wife and mother of two young girls, teaching grammar school in Orange County, California, I crashed into a tragic fork in the road. My fifteen-year-old daughter, Tara, was killed in a car accident. Tragedy ripped my whole life apart, filling in the holes with numbness, anger, and pain.

At such a profound level of grief, it would have been easy for me to slip into a deep and debilitating depression; but with time and deep reflection, this tragedy became an opportunity to create a new, more joyful path for my life. My student consciousness propelled me to learn how to grow through the pain of my tremendous loss while staying connected to my husband, Kirk, and my younger daughter, Deanna.

In 1993, Kirk and I opened Tara's Angels, a retail gift store with the theme of angels, which our daughter had loved. This little store also became a place of teaching, sharing, and miraculous healing that would honor Tara in ways we could never have imagined. We were featured on national television shows and on the cover of *People* magazine.

After six years, my experiences at Tara's Angels inspired me to use my teaching skills in the ministry. Kirk and I became ordained ministers and established the Center for Spiritual Living Orange County in San Juan Capistrano, California.

My daughters have been my greatest teachers. Tara taught me about spirituality and eternal life. Deanna has expanded my awareness about the sacredness of our world and sustaining it through our thoughts and how we live. Deanna keeps me on the path of conscious awareness and diversity. Her experiences have made her my best and most treasured resource in expanding my own green thinking.

Here is what Deanna has to say about her background:

> *Since I was a teenager, I have had remarkable opportunities to participate in experiential education courses and to study abroad. My studies have taken me all over the United States and around the world. I've lived in Southern Africa where I studied ecology and worked with endangered cheetah populations. I studied cultural geography and sustain-*

able agriculture in Hawaii, where I received my permaculture design certificate and teaching certificate. Permaculture is a total design science that includes food, waste, water, shelter and energy. I did postgraduate work in Canada where I worked with First Nations people and sustainable forestry.

Today I am an environmental educator, ecological designer, and organic chef and gardener, living, writing about, and teaching the art and science of sustainable living. I'm interested in the human connection to the natural world and how to design sustainable human habitats where people coexist peacefully. I'm further interested in the intersection of environmental and social sustainability and conscious entrepreneurship. I teach courses on permaculture design, nature awareness, organic cooking, and ecological gardening, and I'm constantly coming up with ideas for new courses.

My quest for learning has also taken me to West Africa, India, Mexico and Canada. I've worked with indigenous cultures in Africa, India, and Canada, exchanging seeds and inspiration and promoting the value of traditional knowledge in an ecologically sustainable culture.

I have a master's degree in ecologically sustainable education from Prescott College and a B.A. in culture, ecology, and sustainable community from New College of California. I live in Southern California, serve as a consultant in green design, own a business called F.L.O.W. Foods using sustainable cuisine and another company, Chocolatl, a raw and organic chocolate superfood company. Today I conduct classes in elementary schools, colleges, at festivals and in community centers around the United States. My topics include biodiesel, sustainable food, gardening, tree-planting, eco-spirituality and permaculture design.

What is Permaculture?

Permaculture is a design science that is based in the observation of nature. Permaculture teaches us how to build natural homes, grow our own food, restore diminished landscapes and ecosystems, catch rainwater, build communities and explore our own inner ecology.

One of the best principles of permaculture is that it takes challenges and transforms them into solutions. Using natural systems as models to design our lives has been done for a long time by our ancestors. Indigenous cultures naturally embodied these concepts for centuries and continue to do so today. Permaculture design science teaches us that:

- Nature works
- Nature is full of solutions
- Nature is always abundant
- There is no such thing as waste
- Stability comes from diversity & strength of relationships
- Everything gardens
- Nature is constantly evolving, changing & growing

Resources:
Regenerative Design Institute: www.regenerativedesign.org
Permaculture Institute: www.permaculture.org

I first learned about Permaculture on the big island of Hawaii, where after backpacking over all of the islands, I lived on a permaculture education farm in a communal setting. It was on the farm and the surrounding jungle that I came to understand and love the deep & complex patterns of nature;

the way the plants & animals live and grow together to form healthy, abundant and interwoven tapestries of life.

There I learned about how to OBSERVE the natural, wild world so that I could interact with it in a way that is empowering and regenerating for all life. Upon observation of natural systems I was able to use them as models and allies for designing abundant & sustainable human landscapes.

I spent my days in Hawaii tending diverse banana gardens, building compost piles, planting seeds, caring for chickens, weeding, maintaining composting toilets, and harvesting fruits, roots & veggies at the height of ripeness to sell at the morning farmers market in town. I learned how to build a house by hand from local materials that would last for years and eventually decompose back into the earth. I see that the time I spent in Hawaii as pivotal in the formation of my values & actions, and my whole life seemed to finally make sense when I was working & living in Hawaii.

My mom and I support one another unconditionally, and one of the best parts of our relationship is learning from one another. I am delighted to serve as her mentor in being green in the same way she has been my spiritual mentor.

Deanna has helped me to understand that being green requires being a student of life. You must be willing to keep learning more about yourself, and examine deeply your own life stories. It asks that you remain curious about how to live the best life, and best of all it asks that you continue to grow.

Personal growth is about striving for wholeness. Although human beings are multifaceted, most people are not "cooking on enough burners," as one of my mentors, renowned psychologist Jean Houston, Ph.D., has wittily pointed out. I believe that work in personal growth lies in bringing the many aspects of yourself into alignment with your own good. What are some of these aspects?

- Work / Career
- Body
- Spirit
- Relationships
- Creativity
- Fun / Play

Often, while you may need work in several areas, there's a particular aspect of your life that is calling out for the most attention. How do you need to grow? What is the perfect expression of your multidimensional self? What is the vision of your life that you'd like to create? This book will help you answer these questions and many others relating to self-exploration and personal expression.

Green happens when infinite creativity meets human potential to create a sustainable development and outcome.

FINDING A HEALING PATH

A few months after Tara's passing, I came to realize that she would not want me to be unhappy the rest of my life. To recover, I had to learn how to take care of and love myself. Growing beyond the pain involved looking at the parts of me that I kept hidden for self-preservation. To triumph over this level of adversity would require that I do more than what I thought was the best I could do.

At Tara's Angels, many people shared their stories of loss and grief. I wanted to offer them a path to healing into a "whole person." But you can't give what you don't have. So I began to learn how to heal, stretch, and grow despite my grief, as I tuned in to my heart, to what I really wanted. In essence, Tara's death jarred me into discovering a healthier way of living.

Until tragedy struck, I had been a productive person who valued personal growth. To be a good schoolteacher you must keep learning, and I always did just that. But I valued myself based on what I did. When my life fell apart, I no longer had my "doing" to value for awhile. I had to learn to value myself simply for who I am. I began to ask myself, how do I get back into alignment with me? The answer was to stop looking to society to validate me and to focus on my inner wisdom. I had to discover the true nature of my being. That shift was a huge gift, which sprang from my desire to be a student of life, no matter how desperate the circumstances.

LEARNING FROM EACH OTHER

We are here to learn and to grow. Over the years, I have learned much from many people's stories and ideas—individuals such as Dr. Wayne W. Dyer, Dr. Jean Houston, Barbara Marx Hubbard, Shirley MacLaine, Mary Manin Morrissey, Marianne Williamson, James Van Praagh, and Oriah Mountain Dreamer. I am excited now to complete the circle by sharing my own story and life lessons to support your growth as well as mine.

> There is an inner urge in our minds to grow,
> to expand, to break down the barriers
> of previous limitations and to
> ever widen our experience.
> JOEL S. GOLDSMITH

□

PIVOTAL TIMING

We live in interesting times in the early twenty-first century. There are so many old paradigms in the world that are breaking down. Changes are going on in government, economics, education, relationships, and the way that society works. As individuals, we need to be seeking new approaches for moving through life. I call these "green intentions." Even though there are many things one can do to become green, the core intention must be at the root of every action first. The process of changing your thoughts and habits can be another story. Let's face it, change is difficult and the purpose of this book is to help you change your thoughts, actions, and habits from the source – where the core intention drives your life. Once you have completed this book, you will have the guidelines and tools necessary to pinpoint and redirect your intention towards a green life.

There is more at stake in being green than the development of your individual path. Your path crosses the paths of others. Your actions may cause many results. Your triumph fuels the triumph of others—something to remember when the going gets tough. Your success may be a sustainable outcome.

Love,
Reverend Sandy

The Green Intention

CHAPTER 1

Setting Your Intention

A Good Design Invites Success

Wherein good design in front makes less work behind.
PERMACULTURE TENET OF DESIGN

If we don't change our direction, we'll wind up
where we're headed.
CHINESE PROVERB

How can we expect to thrive, be joyful and healthy, if we don't design our lives to be great? How we design our lives is important. One of the first rules of design is to begin with a good plan. The right design at the beginning of any project makes less work at the end. The same is true for life. When we orient ourselves in the right direction and set a strong intention, the Universe conspires for our good.

A good design when building a home is to start by orienting the south side with the arch of the sun. In so doing, we allow nature's light to heat and cool our home properly, to provide an efficient environment in which to live. In our personal lives, good design must intentionally and purposefully align our mind, body, and spirit with the creative energy of the Universe to nurture a healthy and peaceful relationship with the environment and others. Life becomes more synchronistic, attuned, healthy, and responsive to change. Good design helps us to thrive.

In the past decade, the word *green* has become much more than a color. It's a symbol of environmental consciousness, because the color has always been associated with nature, healthy living, and growth. The Green Movement has sprung from a wide variety of Green Parties around the globe comprised of people and businesses that emphasize ecology, design, nonviolence, social justice, and grassroots democracy. Green has become a verb as we learn to *green* our homes and offices, and, ultimately, our own lives.

What does it mean to green your life? On the surface, you might think it means to recycle or to purchase, cook, and eat organic foods and beverages, or to turn the lights out every time you leave a room even after you have converted your lightbulbs to save energy. But think for a moment about greening your life at a deeper and broader level. Are you truly thriving now? Are you creating success or fear? What path are you on? Now think about where you want to be. What do you visualize? What do you want to do? How are you serving the world? How do you want to get to your vision?

We are the designers of our own lives, and ultimately of the world around us. All of us have the inherent ability to identify and envision our possibilities. I believe that what we think creates our reality, what we plant into the fertile soil of our minds will in time return to us as our experiences. When we plant good thoughts and follow them with positive actions, we cultivate joy—and that's what I mean by "It's so easy being green."

Several years ago, a stranger named Michelle Spieker walked into an open house at our home which was for sale in Capistrano Beach. We were not at home at the time. She saw our family portrait on the wall alongside a framed cover of *People* magazine featuring a photo of Kirk and me with the caption, "Touched by an Angel." As Michelle looked at our pictures, she proclaimed with deep intention that she wanted to meet these people and get to know them. She planted that intention in the fertile soil of her mind and listened to the guidance of spirit to help that intention grow. She was guided to drop off her book, *The Cherished Self*, at our Tara's Angels store to see if we wanted to carry it. The manager promised to give it to me when I returned from lunch.

We used to receive many books from authors wanting us to carry them, but with my busy schedule I didn't have time to read many of the books. For some reason, most likely Michelle's powerful intention, this book captured my attention and I stayed up very late that night reading it. I called her the next day and said I would love to carry her book in our store. It quickly became one of our best sellers.

Today Michelle and I are deep and special friends. Besides being an integral part of our spiritual center, her family has become like our family. I was blessed to be there for the birth of her daughter, Ella, and she has become a mentor and great support for Deanna. Out of her strong intention has grown a special friendship and love.

To design a magnificent life, to be the essence of what it means to be green, you must attune to the Truth of your being, your Divine self. With the guidance in this book, you'll delve deeply into your Soul and unearth a vision of your best life—a life based on what feeds your Spirit and aligns with true purpose. Assess the conditions that you have been growing into—the inherited fear, blame, victimhood, and self-doubt. Tap into, understand, and create a vision for your potential and then use that vision to create an empowered life—a *green* life.

**Are you ready to get started? The first step will be
setting your intention...**

WHY BEGIN WITH INTENTION?

We live in a creative Universe which will support the goals we set. However, as human beings, we have been given free will. We can choose whether or not to be creative with our lives. When we aren't creative in this way, we live basically the same day over and over and over again. Our journey begins with setting our *Intention* to be open to moving in the direction of our purpose and dreams. In other words, we begin by setting our intention on greening our life.

Greening one's life requires both intention and commitment. Green means growth. In human life, that means you must expend the energy to move beyond your comfort zone. Staying safe by limiting yourself to your comfort zone is not living green. It is focusing on your small, human self, the self that wants to always feel comfortable. This small-self hangs on desperately to the ordinary, and it is driven by the Ego which seeks approval from the world rather than answers from Spirit.

> Leave all thoughts of the world you knew before.
> Let your soul take you where you long to be.
> ERICH FROMM

☐

In contrast to the ego, our Spirit is made up of creative energy, and it keeps growing. Its desire is to move toward freedom, greater understanding, and enlightenment. And so this book encourages thinking from the Spirit—operating from what I call *soul-level thinking*. This spiritual perspective will allow you to grow because you'll have a higher purpose in mind. Soul-level thinking recognizes that there are no mistakes, just further opportunities for growth and expansion. If you allow yourself to stumble at times, viewing life through soulful eyes will help you get unstuck. Then you can move to the green edge, where every day will grow creatively out of the previous one.

SETTING YOUR INTENTION:
A GOOD DESIGN INVITES SUCCESS

Some people say that it's not easy being green, but there couldn't be a better time to be green. With the looming economic crisis & environmental destruction, it is easy to be overwhelmed. This is an opportunity for the systems that are not sustainable to fall away and to reimagine & redesign them in a way that restores balance and grows true wealth. This is a time to act on our intentions.

One of my most profound teachers, Lynne Twist, once told me that energy flows toward clarity, boldness, & authenticity. The clarity sometimes is the hardest part, but is essential in taking action toward success, growth and change.

I started my business, Chocolatl (a raw, organic, fair trade chocolate company), just before the economy took a downturn. Despite the hard time, I remained committed to the highest quality ingredients, 100% biodegradable packaging and grassroots customer education & marketing. I was able to get a small loan from some friends to start up Chocolatl, and after a year or so of doing business, we were doing well, but needed more financing to make it work.

Was it even going to work? I was in a position to either close the business or dive in deeper and go full-steam ahead. I met with a financial consultant who said that with the proper plans & actions, my business was definitely capable of being profitable in a reasonable amount of time. After that was clear I had to step out and ask for what I wanted: like-minded people to invest in a fast-growing, values-driven company. I received a lot of community support for my commitment to quality & sustainability, and I was able to bring in partners that were in full alignment with the vision, loved our products and have since been a pleasure to work with.

We are in fact on a growing edge of consumer values of sustainability, holistic health, and social fairness. The saying "don't think you are on the right track just because it's a well-beaten path" reminds us that the cheapest, most popular and convenient path is not necessarily the most significant or influential.

What do you want to grow?

Take charge of your life by consciously choosing to set your intention on growth. At the same time, make the decision to operate from a spiritual inner directedness to foster your growth. Take responsibility for greening your dreams carefully. The list below gives you some examples of how a community can support your intention to grow. Observe your community to determine the best route for you.

- Passion
- Commitment
- Creativity
- Inspiration
- Ecological Sustainability
- Fairness
- Positive communication
- Good relationships
- Care of the Earth and others
- Regeneration

- Cooperation
- Quality
- Action
- Health in mind and body
- Awareness
- Diversity and interdependence
- Using nature as a guide
- Sustainable growth
- Using renewable resources

Resources:
Lynne Twist: www.soulofmoney.org

MY INTENTION TO HEAL

Perhaps you were drawn to this step of setting a conscious intention on growth because of a subtle disquiet in your heart. Or maybe you were propelled here by a tremendous loss. My most powerful intention was set after Tara's death. I began searching because I just couldn't look at life in the same way anymore.

Reaching out to find a way through my grief, I saw that others were stuck—*for years*—in the pain of losing a loved one. However, the love I shared with Tara was so strong that I knew she would not want me to live a life of unhappiness and pain. So I set my intention on *healing*. I did everything I could to rise above the deep, excruciating pain of my loss and reconnect to life with a new depth of compassion and understanding. It was a long journey shared with my husband, Kirk, and younger daughter, Deanna, and it brought me to a place of great purpose, and even greater love.

Tara's death was so sudden, so unexpected—something I could never have imagined happening in my life. My pain was so intense that at times I had to pull over to the side of the road and weep from sheer despair. What I didn't realize at the time was that life was giving me the opportunity to reconnect with my heart through grief. And as I journeyed through grief, my heart told me I needed to redefine myself. I knew my love for Tara was eternal, as hers was for me. I became aware that part of my grief was about losing my identity as Tara's mom in this physical world. By setting my intention on healing, I discovered I could begin focusing on my identity as Deanna's mom and Kirk's wife, as well as embracing new roles as an entrepreneur and minister. My intention to heal always pulled me forward.

Grief's causes take many forms—the death of a loved one, the loss of a romantic relationship, the end of a job or career, a terrible financial burden, or the announcement of a health diagnosis—anything that rips a life apart. You might find yourself in need of a dramatic change to satisfy a deep longing. When you choose to heal and learn how to move beyond pain and its accompanying frustrations, you invariably gain greater understanding of yourself.

It takes a lot of courage to release the familiar and seemingly secure, to embrace the new. But there is no real security in what is no longer meaningful.

ALAN COHEN

□

WHAT KEEPS PEOPLE STUCK

We are often stuck in our old ways or in limited options because we're immobilized by fear of changing. Here are three common fears that stop us from moving forward.

1. **Fear of losing the approval of others.** In the physical world, we are judged by how our life appears to other people. Pressure to keep up appearances can put us in a rut. We may begin to talk with others about changing, but then be discouraged because they want us to remain the same. How many times have you observed a couple growing apart because one person changed and the other person couldn't accept the "new" partner? In contrast, the Spirit world is nonjudgmental. Spirit knows that we are here to grow constantly, and that the physical aspects of life are ever-changing.

2. **Fear of making mistakes.** At times we get stuck because we want to do everything the right way. But during a growth spurt, mistakes are inevitable because you're moving in unknown

territory. Instead of trying to avoid mistakes by doing nothing, recognize that every situation holds seeds for personal and spiritual growth. Our mistakes offer opportunities to learn, grow, gain insights into ourselves, and develop new skills.

3. **Fear of our own greatness.** Even when getting glimpses of a better way of being, perhaps of our Divine Self, we may be leery of moving toward this vision. Why? One reason is that we fear the envy that embracing our greatness might invoke. This fear can keep us from allowing ourselves to stand out, wishing instead to remain unnoticed as part of the herd. It can keep us stuck in mediocrity. But what if we used our successes to motivate others? What if we shared a beautiful home, loving relationship, and the other fruits of hard work? Remember, attacks are a cry for help and love.

If fear can immobilize us, how do we move beyond fear into hope and excitement about the future? People can make this shift by having faith in aspects of the Universe that we cannot see. What it takes is knowing that there's something larger going on in the Universe—more than we can physically sense.

At the time we lost Tara, I was in the teaching profession that I had been in for twenty years. I had to look at my life and see if what I was doing still made sense, or was there something greater calling to grow through me? The answer was YES! There was a new idea wanting to emerge through me. I could not see the extent of it, which we usually cannot when a new idea is born. However, I felt the pull to complete my teaching career and step into a new expression of myself.

Since my life had changed so greatly, I no longer fit in my old life and it was time to create a new one. I needed time to meditate, envision, and see what came forth as I allowed a space for newness.

At first my intention was simply to do something new in my life that was in alignment with my new emerging being.

When you look at a baby, or think about the way the planets hang so perfectly in outer space, do you consider that there are greater things going on than what you presently understand? When considering this bigger picture relative to your daily life, you won't feel intimidated and overwhelmed by the inevitable changes. You know you're part of a dynamic Universe, which always supports you in whatever you are experiencing in the physical realm.

> The most destructive element in the human mind is fear...Only when we are no longer afraid do we begin to live.
> DOROTHY THOMPSON

□

THE ROLE OF ATTENTION

When we design our life with the bigger picture in mind, everything unfolds holistically. When our life is random and without design, we become fragmented, sacrificing our full potential and wasting precious energy. We must consistently pause and make sure we are in alignment with our intention, that where we place our attention is feeding our design for life.

Remember This: Setting an intention is about making an overall commitment.

Attention is a tool we use to make deliberate choices about what gets our focus at any given time in our lives. When you live an intentional life, your attention is focused on what fosters desired growth. What diminishes you, keeps you stuck, or appears to encourage growth on the surface but doesn't serve your deeper needs and desires, is ignored.

Are the daily choices you're making about where you place your attention—the seeds of your intention—drawing the growth you seek to manifest in your life? Could you be planting the same seeds in the fertile soil of your potentiality and expecting a different life experience to grow? I continued teaching as I let a new idea grow in me. I noticed that because I made room for newness, new ideas and possibilities presented themselves. Twenty years previously when I had set my intention and attention on getting a teaching job when they were scarce in California, my clarity of intention to step into something new drew the people and situations to me that allowed me to get a job teaching when it seemed impossible.

In every moment, we have the opportunity to redefine our lives. When you use the tool of Attention and focus your activities toward a goal, the Law of Attraction draws it to you. Energetically you pull the experience you want from the Universe. *Attention matters.*

The Law of Attraction: Like attracts like

DOING YOUR PART

Moving your life forward requires preparation. As you become aware of where attention is focused, notice the necessary details related to the "getting ready" stage. Even with powerful spiritual principles at work, you still need to do your part.

John Wooden led UCLA to ten national basketball championships and became a sports legend. Wooden likes to point out that success in life starts "from the socks up." He talks about how many talented basketball players end up sitting on the bench because of painful blisters. These blisters are the result of something as simple as not putting their socks on properly before putting on their shoes. Similarly, certain simple details of your game of growth could put you "on the bench" if you don't take care of them in a timely manner.

Details were part of what made U2 rock star Bono a spiritual hero in 2005. Bono worked tirelessly to secure $40 billion in debt relief for poverty-stricken African nations. In order to complete his successful mission, Bono paid attention to the details. He learned the specifics of the AIDs crisis in Africa — knowledge that prompted those in power to take his effort seriously. Bono garnered the support of the World Bank, the International Monetary Fund, congressional representatives, United Nations officials and others — not exactly the company you'd expect a rocker to keep, nor people who are easily impressed. Bono's attention to detail made a difference that ultimately saved thousands of lives.

Later chapters will deal more directly with the issue of taking action. For now, just keep in mind that moving forward takes more than merely having an intention; but intention is a beginning.

> It's not good enough for things to be planned—they still
> need to be done; for the intention to be a reality,
> energy has to be launched into operation.
> WALT KELLY

☐

Green Intention Affirmations: Connecting to the Divine

It takes courage to green your own life, because the ego wants to cling to the status quo. Learn to consciously unhook yourself from ego-based consciousness in order to shift to a spiritual.

Affirmations are an excellent way to maintain and strengthen your connection to Spirit. The following affirmations may help in letting go of ego and embracing your Divine self. In addition to meditating on these, copy them onto colorful index cards to place around your home or room.

I was created with a purpose as part of a Divine plan.

I am a part of the Universal energy.

I am open to growing into my Divine self.

*I am open to allowing the Universe to assist me
in unfolding my good.*

I will do my part.

I am not alone in my journey.

When you feel deserted and alone, life gets difficult, but when you're aware of your connection to the Universe, you can open your heart and mind in order to be supported by Spirit. Practice using these green affirmations to keep you in the flow of life.

Contemplate the following affirmation every morning:

There is opportunity in this day.

This perspective helps you switch from viewing the day's responsibilities as drudgery to seeing them as opportunities to connect joyfully with yourself, others, and life. For instance, when my home in San Juan Capistrano was for sale, I decided not to resent the effort I had to make in order to keep it presentable for potential buyers, nor to begrudge all the time Kirk and I had to spend looking for a new home. Instead, I chose to view these activities through the lens of opportunity; I saw the potential of creating something new and wonderful in my life—a new, beautiful home that I could enjoy with my family and friends. This attitude shifted my energy from negative to positive—to an experience of expansion and abundance.

Remember This: Always know that a greater good is available to you. Adopting an expectancy of good through positive affirmations will increase your excitement about living. As your excitement rises, others will be inspired by your positive attitude.

THE ART OF PATIENCE

In making a commitment to growth, summon your patience. This kind of change takes time. The Universe has its own sense of timing, which we don't always comprehend. A basic principle to keep in mind is that life unfolds and evolves at exactly the right pace. This is often slower than we wish. However, getting worked up over the pacing won't speed things along.

Another way to grow more patient is to notice and appreciate the change that *is* occurring. Look for the little changes that move you forward. Notice opportunities to develop more possibilities because the mind is focused on growth, rather than delay. You'll likely recognize even more chances to move ahead.

Patience is a learned art. It comes when you believe that ultimately, the Universe wants the best for you—I call this your "good"—and it supports you in cultivating your vision of joy. Patience makes the journey more pleasant, because you are more present and can enjoy gifts as they come.

Everything comes gradually and at its appointed hour.
OVID

□

GROWTH EXERCISE

Developing a Vision: What Do You Really Want?

1) How to be patient on the journey

Put down this book. Get your journal or a piece of paper and write out some ways to be more patient about your planned journey of growth.

2) Opening to the Vision

In the next several chapters, we'll be pushing through barriers that might keep you from pursuing a vision of your best life, including thoughts of unworthiness, leftover emotional baggage, and so forth. Then, we'll focus on creating a specific life vision. But right now, let's get started by thinking generally about what that vision might look like. That way, you'll be ready to do deeper work with this when you get further into the book.

How does someone develop a vision of their life so that it's in alignment with their true self? It helps to ask yourself questions that allow you to consider various outcomes.

Take a deep breath. Now take another one. And now ask yourself, *If time, money, and resources were not an issue, what would I be doing right now?* Listen to your heart for the answer, not your head. This isn't about what others want from you (family, business associates, etc.). This is about what *you* really, *really* want. Spend a few minutes writing down the answers.

Next question: *What is keeping me from doing this?* Write out the answers that come from your heart.

Keep these questions and answers close as you read the next three chapters.

Your divine nature is there from the beginning of your evolution in human form. It is the real you—but in the beginning it is unawakened.

MILDRED NORMAN

☐

WHAT'S NEXT?

Unless you heal your thoughts of unworthiness, you will sabotage the growth intention. The next chapter will help further open the receptive channels for your good.

> Most of the shadows of this life are caused by
> standing in one's own sunshine.
> RALPH WALDO EMERSON

☐

CHAPTER 2

Thoughts of Unworthiness

Composting Your Unwanted Beliefs and Reusing the Ones You Want

As a single footstep will not make a path on the earth,
so a single thought will not make a pathway in the mind.
To make a deep and physical path, we walk again and again.
To make a deep mental path, we must think over and over
the kind of thoughts we wish to dominate our lives.

HENRY DAVID THOREAU

Real education consists of drawing out the best of yourself.

MAHATMA GANDHI

Environmentally conscious beings choose to use nontoxic products in their homes. They are aware of the adverse effects of toxic products, not only on the people in the home, but to the environment at large. Toxic products can have harmful effects on people and on the planet. The same is true of toxic thoughts. Toxic thoughts include those of fear, lack, unworthiness, shame, guilt, and vengeance.

We live in an abundant and infinite Universe, so why do our lives sometimes feel deprived and limited? One of the problems in Western society is people often feel unworthy of the good that is available to them. We think, "I am not enough." Nothing could be further from the truth of who we are. When you are seduced by thoughts and feelings of unworthiness, immediately get on the track to thinking about your natural right to abundance. As a child of this, you are worthy of its gifts.

The first step to shedding this belief in unworthiness is awareness. Be aware that your thoughts are who you are now. Recognize that your belief in your unworthiness naturally limits your good. Work with the ideas and practices in this chapter to eliminate any negative self-perception, now and always.

When we believe we are unworthy, we act accordingly. Kirk and I painfully experienced this phenomenon in 1988 when we moved our family from Los Angeles to Orange County, California.

A LIFE-CHANGING MOVE

In 1988, when Kirk and I transplanted our family to the upscale community of Laguna Hills, it appeared we had finally achieved the perfect life. We bought a big, beautiful home on a large lot that boasted a gorgeous view of the ocean. We had two sparkling new automobiles, a Volvo and a sports car. Kirk was a successful mortgage broker. Our beautiful daughters, Tara and Deanna, ages ten and eight, adjusted quickly to the new locale, made new friends, and loved their school.

With all this apparent joy, Kirk and I still felt unworthy of the good life. On some level, we believed we didn't deserve this wonderful experience. As a reflection of our feelings of unworthiness, Kirk suddenly lost his job. Stuck in the catch-22 of being over- or underqualified for available positions, he ended up out of work for a year. We had to sell our gorgeous new home and move into a smaller, more affordable one.

Kirk and I live on a roller coaster, not a merry-go-round. We've experienced amazing highs and lows. The year that we moved to Orange County took us from peak to valley, with lots of butterflies and nausea along the way. We went from living what we thought was the perfect life to letting it all go. But somehow during that time, we were guided to find a new church — right out of the phone book. We discovered the Capistrano Valley Church of Religious Science. Soon our family's spirituality went from being a peripheral activity to the nucleus of our lives.

When our life appears to reflect unworthiness, we must do some composting to find nutrients — the innate potential and gifts hidden in the scraps of garbage, or bad experiences that find their way into our souls. My family's experience of losing our dream home taught us that we needed to activate our trust in life's learning processes — and in our faith. We stayed with the Capistrano Valley Church until we knew we wanted to establish our own spiritual center in 1999.

Remember This: Whatever you put your attention on will grow and expand.

We feel unworthy when we give problems tremendous power over our lives instead of focusing on simple solutions. All we really need to do is *compost our unworthy thoughts and focus on solutions.* If you're focusing on feeling unworthy, you will have many opportunities to feel that way. If you feel unworthy, you might:

- Lose your job
- End a relationship
- Experience financial insecurity
- Become seriously ill

Focusing on solutions requires us to place our perceived unworthiness into a compost pile, allowing it to decompose and return to its natural state of worthiness. We are worthy of solutions because the natural state of the universe includes solving and resolving. More importantly, we are worthy of greater potential, way above and beyond what looks impossible right now. Kirk and I took a step toward embracing our innate worthiness when we dialed the phone number to get information about the church that became our bridge to a better life.

Spiritual practices—methods, techniques, and habits that let you experience the reality of your spiritual life—are invaluable in living your best life.

Reduce, Reuse, Recycle

We can all be part of our change for good if we change our habits and make a few practices part of our daily living.

Reduce, Reuse, Recycle

Where to begin to take steps toward a more conscious lifestyle? Think of the big picture, but don't get overwhelmed. Pick the low-hanging fruit first! This means, for example, before installing a solar panel system on your home, change all of your light bulbs in your house first. Get a home energy audit (newleafamerica.com), and purchase energy efficient appliances, first.

It is about being connected to the THINGS that we use; understanding where they come from and where they are going. Having an understanding of the "embodied energy" of items and resources and the life cycle of a product helps immensely in making conscious choices.

Reduce

Simply speaking, waste is anything discarded, rejected, surplused, abandoned, or otherwise released into the environment in a way that could have an impact on that environment. Waste prevention, or "source reduction," means consuming and throwing away less. It includes: purchasing durable, long-lasting goods; seeking products and packaging that are as free of toxics as possible; redesigning products to use less raw material in production, have a longer life, or be used again after its original use.

Make small lifestyle changes to reduce energy consumption, like conserving hot water, turning off lights, unplugging all electrical devices when not in use (television, computer, phone, etc), and purchasing materials that are recycled. Set yourself up for success, and find ways of daily changing habits & patterns that can create big change.

Reuse

Reusing items — by repairing them, donating them to charity and community groups, or selling them — also reduces waste. Reusing products, when possible, is even better than recycling because the item does not need to be reprocessed before it can be used again.

Before you toss something into the trash, think: Can this be re-used, re-sold, or re-cycled? I reuse paper, plastic & cloth bags by storing them in obvious, convenient places and in my car as well. And I don't beat myself up if I forget my bag, because this is not very often.

Before you buy a new car/guitar/computer/phone/weed-wacker/shovel/ car tire/etc, look for a used one. Particularly in this economy, we can often find things that are less expensive and in excellent condition used. For example, all of the cars I've owned have been used, and when I want a new toy, like a new surfboard, a kitchen appliance, a musical instrument or a garden tool, I look for them used instead of new. I find them online or in the paper, always for a cheaper price and in great condition, especially in this economy.

Recycle

Recycling turns materials that would otherwise become waste into valuable resources. In addition, it generates a host of environmental, financial, and social benefits. Materials like glass, metal, plastics, and paper are collected, separated and sent to facilities that can process them into new materials or products.

Recycling is one of the best environmental success stories of the late 20th century. Every year recycling and composting takes millions and millions of tons of material away from landfills and incinerators. This number continues to increase yearly. Let's continue to do our part for good.

Finally, recycling of food into compost, of packaging and paper definitely needs to be second nature to us! At my house, we recycle all of our food scraps. Some of our food goes to our chickens, some goes in our worm bin, and some goes into the soil to be decomposed by fungus, insects & bacteria.

Small Tips for Big Change:
- **Compost** your food scraps
- **Read Labels** before buying anything, and if you don't know what something is, inform yourself
- **ALWAYS reuse paper**, and when purchasing paper from the office store, MAKE SURE that it is 100% post consumer recyled, or "tree-free."
- **Know how to handle household waste.** Is it recyclable? Is it household waste? Toxic to dispose of?
- **Reuse** paper, plastic & cloth bags.

Resources:
New Leaf America: www.newleafamerica.com
Green Earth office supply: www.greenearthofficesupply.com
Green Nest: www.greennest.com

EMPOWERMENT BY NATURE

Nature has the power to grow into its potential. Nature is intrinsically worthy of becoming all it can be. Tapping into the power of nature is a helpful spiritual practice for overcoming feelings of unworthiness. Consider starting a routine of taking regular walks along the beach or hikes in the woods or the mountains. Even a stroll through the neighborhood can work if you focus on nature instead of stucco or concrete. While you're outdoors, allow yourself to feel and absorb nature's radiant energy. Or instead of nature walks, try the following practice, one that I do from time to time to revitalize my spirit and remind myself about my inherent worthiness.

Go outdoors, and look for something in nature that attracts you—the strength of a tree, the beauty of a flower, or the density of a boulder. Then take your hand and place it upon or beside the item you've chosen. Feel the energy and power of it. Then imagine that energy entering your hand. Next, take your hand and hold it over your heart. Visualize nature's energy entering into your heart, and spreading throughout your entire body. Finally, place your hand back near the item from nature, and send it gratitude for sharing its energy with you.

Nature is an infinite resource for relearning the lesson of your worthiness. It's a place to go when your energy is low. *Be green*—make nature your ally and you will realize its power and energy are always available to you.

LIVING WITH GRATITUDE

Living in a state of perpetual gratitude is a practice that can quickly transform a sense of what I call "not enoughness" into a feeling of "Oh, how rich I am!" Instead of focusing your attention on what's missing—perfect body, superhero energy, money to burn—think about what you have—a sunny day, a delicious meal, enough money to meet your needs—and be grateful. Reinforce this positive perspective by jotting down your current riches in your journal.

The power of an attitude of gratitude came to my mind again and again during my trip to Ghana, West Africa, in 2005. I traveled with a group led by Brother Ishmael Tetteh, Founder and Spiritual Director of the Etherean Mission in Ghana. The Etherean Mission is a trans-denominational metaphysical organization dedicated to self-awareness and the study of the natural sciences. Brother Ishmael has delivered his message of world peace over the past twenty-nine years, empowering thousands of lives from Africa, to Germany, to the United Kingdom and now to the United States.

During the visit, I learned that Ghana is a very poor country financially, but is very rich in spirit and a sense of having enough. The Ghanaian people are kind and generous. They dress beautifully and stand tall, even in the poorest areas. They are very rich in what they do have—a sense of personal pride and genuine human warmth. The men who come to iron your clothes, the women who work so hard in the orphanages, and the people you meet in the streets all seem so joyous and grateful to be alive. They are ready to smile and share their love. I asked one woman why it was that all the people seemed so happy when they had so little. She replied that America is rich in money, Ghana is rich in spirit. I left Ghana realizing that we have much to learn from its people about being grateful for what we do have.

Stay Stuck or Be Pulled Forward?

Have you ever been so stuck in the muck of your life that you couldn't see the higher ground right there within reach? At times like these, you tend to feel only the heavy weight of your feelings of unworthiness, which are generated by negative thoughts. How different it feels, in contrast, when you affirm your worthiness by stating positive intentions. By making that better choice, you are pulled forward in a positive direction via your vision of a brighter future.

Do your thoughts keep you down or lift you up? Negative thoughts can create manifestations of unworthiness in your life because they drain your power, strength, and energy. With imagination and creativity, you can work on moving toward your highest potential. Try repeating this as a daily practice: *I live in the now, but also keep a vision of my posi-*

tive intentions running at the same time—like a dual image screen on a TV. Throughout the day, I remind myself of my wonderful intentions for the day and the future.

Empower yourself and move beyond a world of ordinary struggle and uncertainty—the world of unworthiness. Instead, attune your thoughts to living up to your worth and potential.

ACKNOWLEDGING YOUR FEELINGS

Embracing worthiness doesn't mean you only experience positive feelings. Life isn't rosy all the time for anyone, no matter how much we'd like to experience only the "ups" and none of the "downs." It's normal to experience feelings of challenge and stress during tough times. You'll want to have a method for recognizing what you're going through emotionally. Otherwise, the feelings will exert themselves in undesirable ways—through a fit of anger, an illness, or general irritability. Having a method for recognizing feelings allows you to be honest about them, but prevents the emotions from running your life.

Effective ways for getting in touch with your feelings include dumping them out onto the pages of your journal, or sharing them with a sympathetic friend who is a good listener. As an accompaniment to journaling, a breath work meditation can help bring feelings into your awareness. Close your eyes and go inside yourself as you breathe in a relaxed manner and ask *What am I feeling in this moment?* Allow the feelings to come up and then pour them out onto the page. Just let it all spill out onto the page where it's safe. I call this practice my "dumping ground." When you finish writing, you can read what you wrote, or not. If not, it can be liberating to tear up the pages.

It's healthy to let the little child inside yourself have a tantrum through journaling. No one will judge you. I developed the habit of using journaling for this purpose after reading Julia Cameron's *The Artist's Way*. Later I conducted workshops based on her book, and found that people felt empowered through journaling their feelings. Every morning I clear myself by releasing my feelings in my journal so I can start the day fresh.

Releasing Feelings through Bodywork

Despite your best efforts, it's likely you will repress some feelings and store them in your body. For instance, have you ever felt tightness in your shoulders when experiencing stress? Purposeful bodywork is a healthy way to let feelings go.

Your choice of bodywork might include Swedish or Shiatsu massage. It could be exercising—a few yoga classes each week or a daily bike ride. It might be sitting in a Jacuzzi and gently rolling your head around on your neck while rubbing your upper back with your fingers.

Working your body in these ways helps release the feelings that are stuck inside. It also supports connecting to your worthiness by allowing you to feel more energized and clear in the present moment.

SURROUNDING YOURSELF WITH POSITIVE PEOPLE

It's been said that we become a composite of the five people we spend the most time with. Because we are so strongly influenced by those around us, it's important to choose people who uplift you and strengthen your energy. You want to be able to think, "I feel empowered by this person."

Take a good look at the people in your inner circle. If they don't empower you, begin to take some steps to draw more positive people into your orbit. Try some new classes, join a spiritual community, and go to other places where positive people gather. Consider people who you would like to get to know better.

There will always be some people who drag you down. Make an effort to limit the amount of time you spend with them. Learn to set some boundaries, even with members of your family.

When we opened our Tara's Angels store many people found it a safe place to share their losses and grief. I found some people were very stuck in their pain and I felt drained and depleted after spending time with them. Part of me felt obligated as a compassionate person to give so much of my time away. I was allowing them to get a hold on me and I became sucked into their pain and suffering. It was starting to affect my health.

One day a woman came in the store and said she had a message from Tara. She said Tara was concerned about my health. If I did not start protecting myself from people's pain and grief I could become very ill. I took what she said to heart and to deepen the message I got a call the same day from a woman in New York who asked if I was willing to hear a message she received from my daughter from the other side. She shared exactly the same message.

I found it necessary not only to surround myself in white light before stepping into difficult situations, but also to limit my time with negative people so I would not be too drained to do the work and share the love that was my clear intention. It was not my responsibility to hold others' pain and grief. My responsibility was to be an example of the possibility of healing if we are open to it and willing to do the work.

When you're around negative people, remember that, like you, they are children of our limitless universe. Somewhere in them, there is good to discover. While they may not be displaying their highest potential right now, know that it's hidden. Though it can be challenging, try to help them connect with their higher selves. And let go when you need to take care of yourself.

Remember This: We all need to take steps to honor ourselves and maintain our happiness. Make conscious choices when it comes to the people in your life.

Using All Your Strength

Sometimes manifesting worthiness requires help or insight from another person. You don't have to do it all alone. There is unlimited power in the universe. Make yourself available to its support. The following story from David J. Wolphe's book Teaching Your Children about God illustrates this point.

A boy and his father were strolling down a road and they came across a large rock. The boy turned to his father and asked, "Do you think if I used all my strength that I could move this rock?" And his father answered, "If you use all your strength, I'm sure you can move it." The boy began to push the rock. Exerting himself as much as he could, he pushed and pushed. The rock did not budge. Discouraged, the boy said to his father, "You were wrong. I can't do it." His father placed his arm around the boy's shoulder and said, "No, son, you didn't use all your strength. You didn't ask me for help."

Don't ignore the rocks and stones along your path. If you need help to remove them, love yourself enough to ask for assistance. You are worthy.

DEVELOP "HEALING EYES"

Adjust perspective by developing "healing eyes" that will cultivate your sense of worthiness. Sometimes, your focus may need to shift from surface thinking to something deeper. Like a volcanic island, your life can consist of much more than what you see on top. Perhaps the seeds of effort that you planted have yet to break through the soil, so you discount the effort altogether. Or current turmoil can make you forget that you even planted the seeds at all. Yet there could be so much potential germinating on a deep level.

Shifting your intention is about abiding expansion. Take off your blinders and expand your range of vision. See all the good that is germinating in your life, and all that you have already developed—despite the obstacles you've faced. There is so much good to acknowledge when you see with "healing eyes."

Give yourself an eye exam and improve your vision!

It sometimes takes the wisdom of another to improve the way we view our possibilities. One such wise person was Doug, a man who had become a counselor after a severe injury and a long stay in a convalescent home. In his counseling work, Doug was often asked to work with especially difficult people. With unconditional love and compassion, he was able to show these people, who had hit rock bottom, that they were still very worthy.

One day Doug got a call to go to a nursing home. A patient named Charlie had recently arrived there, and he would not open up with anyone. The patient was despondent because both of his legs had been amputated due to blood clots. He felt his life was over. Charlie was only forty-two, and had been an active runner who competed in marathons.

Doug's first visit turned out to be brief, but he saw how depressed Charlie was. Amazingly, Charlie agreed to see Doug again. The next time, Doug brought Frank along, another man who was also staying at the nursing home. A still-despondent Charlie growled at the two men as they entered: "Why are you here? Do you like seeing a cripple?" Frank explained that he wanted Charlie to write for his sports newsletter. Charlie spat back: "What's the matter? Is something wrong with your hands?" Frank quietly answered, "As a matter of fact, I have no hands at all." Frank explained that he had been born without limbs. He showed Charlie that his arms were actually prosthetic limbs. When Charlie told him that he felt sorry for him, Frank replied, "Why should you feel sorry for me? I don't. This is how I was meant to be."

In the conversation that followed, Charlie broke down and cried. He apologized for his bad behavior. And during the course of that afternoon with Frank and Doug, Charlie's attitude changed. Charlie and Frank went on to work on the newsletter together. And Charlie later admitted that it was Frank's attitude about his own situation that allowed him to see himself and his possibilities in a new light.

Sometimes connecting to our worthiness is simply about connecting to others.

COMPOST THOUGHTS OF UNWORTHINESS

Embracing our worthiness is more than a one-time task. Once we see our worthiness, we must continue to compost the unwanted thoughts that sprout up from time to time. In this work, it helps to not believe everything the world tells you, and even what you tell yourself. Negative thoughts of unworthiness can be planted in our minds through the influence of others in addition to positive thoughts of worthiness. Self-doubt can spring from your own fear and ignorance.

Composting

Another form of recycling is composting. Composting recycles organic household and yard waste into an extremely useful soil-like material called humus. Examples are fruits, vegetables and yard clippings. Ultimately this permits the return of needed organic matter and nutrients into the foodchain and reduces the amount of "green" waste going into landfills. Composting is nature's way of recycling organic waste into new soil, which can be used in vegetable and flower gardens, landscaping, and many other applications. It provides nutrients to the soil, increases beneficial soil organisms (e.g., worms and centipedes), suppresses certain plant diseases, reduces the need for fertilizers and pesticides and protects soils from erosion.

As you identify and separate the negative, critical, harmful thoughts that accumulate in your mind, you are taking the first step to compiling a mental compost that reduces the wasteful components and salvages the nutrients to reaffirm your worthiness.

When your sense of worthiness is challenged by others or yourself, question the opposing viewpoint. Sometimes people are wrong. Sometimes we are wrong about our own potential. Consider the story of Olympic athlete Roger Bannister, a man who forever changed the world's view about what was possible.

In the early 1950s, the record speed for running a mile was a little faster than four minutes. At the time, people said this was as fast as the human body could perform, and that breaking the established record was an impossible feat.

Track star Roger Bannister, a medical student at St. Mary's in London, believed he could run a mile in under four minutes. And he was right. On May 6, 1954, Bannister sped across the finish line at 3:59.4. Then something surprising happened. After years of the record speed hovering just above four minutes, other athletes began to beat Bannister's record. In fact, an astounding twenty-two runners did this fairly soon afterwards, for a total of sixty-six times. The impossible became possible — repeatedly.

When you have doubts about worthiness, try acting as if you believe it. What possibilities could you manifest now? What self-imposed limits could you break through?

THE ROLE OF PRAYER AND MEDITATION

Expanding our vision of ourselves can also require that we activate faith — believe in the power of the Universe, a power beyond ourselves. Using meditation and prayer can help you connect with the higher energies of the Universe.

During meditation, you enter a receptive mode for receiving higher energy. Becoming quiet and still, you enter the empty space within to welcome the Universe's infinite intelligence.

In contrast, prayer is more active. In order to pray you must immediately lift yourself to a higher plane to greet the creative force of the Universe. You extend yourself by aligning your energy with the energy of the higher power. It's impossible to pray from an unworthy place because a natural uplifting is part of the prayer process.

Whenever you want to deepen a sense of your worthiness, turn to an affirmation that connects with your soul.

Green Intention Affirmations: Worthiness

*I choose to stop and take time to savor
the wonder of this moment.*

*I clear my mind of any thoughts that limit my availability to
the ever-present Good.*

*I uplift my vision to truly see the beauty and perfection
of the world.*

*As life unfolds before me, I see this world as a purposeful
and lovely place.*

I know that everyone and everything is part of a Divine Plan.

I see Good everywhere.

*I have a calm, inward knowing of my oneness with all life and
the Infinite Intelligence that is the essence and energy of all
things.*

This energy is my life.

My awareness awakens me to knowing that I am worthy of love and peace;

I am worthy of receiving my Good.

As I accept and claim abundance and joy for my life, I readily share it with others.

Thank you, God, for the rich, wonderful, and supportive world in which we live.

I consciously replace thoughts of what I might lack with an awareness of all I have to offer.

Out of clutter, find simplicity.
From discord, find harmony.
In the middle of difficulty
lies opportunity.

ALBERT EINSTEIN

□

We have a choice to either try to stay where we are or to continue to evolve. Listen to the call within and expand your vision of yourself.

WHAT'S NEXT?

Sometimes we work hard on our worthiness, but life doesn't change for the better. We ask ourselves, *What do I need to let go of?* You must make room in your life for the good, in much the same way you do spring cleaning, letting go of what you no longer need in order to make room for the new. Chapter 3 will explore clearing the clutter in our mind so that new positive possibilities can enter.

New Possibilities

Every Problem Holds the Solution

Everyone has to learn to think differently,
bigger, to open to possibilities.

OPRAH WINFREY

We have more possibilities available in each moment
than we realize.

THICH NHAT HANH

LET GO. Just thinking about those two words makes you feel lighter, doesn't it? Chapter 3 highlights letting go, clearing those things you no longer need or which may not be serving you. In addition to allowing new possibilities to emerge, this clearing helps you discover what you really want.

The work of revealing possibilities and solutions requires creating space on many levels of your life, both physically (with possessions, relationships, etc.) and non-physically (with thinking, beliefs, and behaviors that don't work in the process of your growth). Habitual or transparent living—unconsciously going through our days as we always have—gets us into trouble. *Awareness* is the key.

Simplicity

Simplicity has deep roots in history and finds expression in all of the world's wisdom traditions. It often denotes beauty, purity or clarity.

Duane Elgin describes Voluntary Simplicity as "living in a way that is outwardly simple and inwardly rich." Personal or Voluntary Simplicity includes decreased consumerism and materialism and valuing ecological responsibility, lower energy consumption & self-sufficiency. This means letting go of what we no longer need to allow room for more meaning in our lives.

We must question our daily actions:

What brings me joy?

Do I really need this in my life?

Does this grow peace and balance, or stress and destruction?

How does this affect my quality of life?

Is this ecologically & socially regenerative or degenerative?

Who's quality of life does this affect?

Who & what are we relying on for this aspect of our life to continue?

Resources:
Duane Elgin

CLEARING YOUR MIND

If your mind is crowded, there's little or no room to tap into your innate potential and magnificence. Clearing your mind is about gaining a wider and higher perspective on life and letting go of thoughts that come from a lower, spirit-diminishing perspective. That adjustment can make a huge difference in lightening your mental and emotional load.

Here's a fun story that illustrates just how heavy your thoughts can become:

A ZEN TALE: THE RIVER CROSSING

Two Chinese Zen monks — an elder and a new devotee — were on a pilgrimage, traveling through the country together. When the two men of the cloth arrived at a riverbank, they noticed a young woman who was unable to cross by herself. Seeing her difficulty, the older monk volunteered to carry the girl to the other side. The younger man stood back and watched in dismay as the elder trudged through the water with the young woman in his arms. Finally the younger man also forged the river and joined the elder and the girl.

The young woman departed with a wave toward the elder, and the monks took off again to continue their journey. However, the younger man, who had been very talkative and full of questions, did not say a single word to the elder for the rest of the day. Finally the two monks arrived at a monastery, where they knew they would be provided with meals as well as beds to sleep in overnight. As they were waiting to be directed to the dining hall, the elder monk said, "What's wrong? Why haven't you spoken to me since we left the river?" The younger man replied, "I'm so ashamed. We're supposed to stay away from women, and I can't believe what you did today!" The elder monk responded, "Is that what's bothering you? I left the girl at the riverbank, but you're carrying her around even now!"

We all have expectations of people and then carry around the burden of resentment when they disappoint us. We hold onto thoughts of how people have wronged us. We can't see that our thoughts are hurting us and our minds are clear to do what needs to be done. It's as if we're hanging onto these things with clenched fists, so we can't grab the good that is coming to us. Instead, we must be conscious in order to be clear and receptive to something new and beautiful.

What mental clutter do you need to let go of?

What do you need to make peace with?

LETTING GO OF FEAR

Part of creating the space for solutions to be revealed is to re-identify yourself with what you are becoming rather than who you have been. As you begin to transform identities, it's common to be afraid when you're forced to move beyond your old comfort zones. Fear makes it hard to continue to let go—of jobs, people, of the many things you may need to release. But when is enough really enough? Instead of listening to fear, listen to your inner voice urging, *Start doing something else.*

You may not be comfortable with what you have, but you know what it is. It's the familiarity factor. You're afraid of not knowing what to do, how to act, how to respond. Your ego wants to know and to control. But your spirit has an urge to be free. Your thinking holds you back. Most of us are afraid of making mistakes. If we don't take the initiative to change on our own, the Universe will pull the rug out from under us so that we have to change.

When Kirk and I had made our big move to Orange County from Los Angeles I had decided to take the leap of faith and quit my sixteen-year elementary teaching career to try my hand at real estate. Kirk and I loved homes and we had bought and sold many of them. In fact, we found moving fun. However, liking houses and being a real estate agent are two very different things.

I am inherently a teacher, not a salesperson. However, I struggled to get my business going until Kirk was let go from what we thought was his very secure job and I was forced to reevaluate my situation. My minister asked me what I did best and I said teach. She advised that I go back to teaching. I didn't want to be a substitute teacher after so many years of being a permanent teacher, and I was told that with my education and years of teaching experience it was unlikely I would get a permanent job because I was too high up on the pay scale.

Kirk was having no luck in finding a job—too qualified, not a fit, you name it. Seeing no other way of supporting our children and our home, I went to the local school district, kicking and screaming, and signed up to be a substitute teacher. Because of my willingness to say yes, against my ego's fight to say no, I opened the door for miracles. The first class I substituted in was a classroom where the teacher had become ill. I substituted for a month and then found out the teacher was not going to be able to return to school that year. Because of the bond I had formed with the principal, the students, and the parents, I was able to take over as the permanent teacher. I remained there for three more years until we lost Tara. It was the most rewarding teaching experience of my life.

A mistake is only a mistake if we don't learn from it. Mistakes are Miracle-Gro fertilizer for greening our spiritual life. Embrace your spirituality and allow life to become an evolutionary process of awakening.

Remember This: Listen to the clear small inner voice urging you on. Take one step at a time. Yes, there's a lot to do, but you can move ahead at a pace that won't make you feel overwhelmed and afraid.

> The moment of surrender is not
> when life is over
> but when life really begins.
> MARIANNE WILLIAMSON

☐

LETTING GO OF PERFECTIONISM

In cultivating joy, you will need to let go of the outmoded habit of perfectionism. When I find myself striving for perfection, I stop and think about what it is that I truly want and need at that moment. Sometimes I don't know the answer. Often, we try to live according to other people's expectations—a recipe for disaster in life's garden. Recognize right here and now that a drive to be perfect may be motivated by the mental tapes of the voice of a parent criticizing you. Parental judgments like "you're not good enough," "do it better," or "be better" can be damaging and paralyzing, even though the original intent might have been to be helpful.

Perfectionism is focusing on unrealistic and unachievable goals. It is based on a belief that unless we're perfect, we're not OK. Perfectionism surfaces when we forget that humans learn and grow through mistakes and imperfections. Individuals caught up in perfectionism invariably experience stress, as well as health problems and emotional imbalance. They often incite negative reactions from others because of their unrealistically high standards.

Perfectionists participate in an intense competition with themselves. Fear of failure, of looking bad, being wrong or being judged governs their actions. If you can identify with this behavior, ask yourself: *What is the worst thing that could happen if I don't do everything perfectly?* Practice leaving some things undone—not as perfect as you might like them to be. Be willing to try something you've never done and to make mistakes in the learning.

While letting go of perfectionism, it's helpful to reinterpret the phrase "striving for excellence." Instead of seeing excellence as perfectionism, try viewing it as the desire to do the very best possible, being willing to do what it takes—mistakes and all—to grow and evolve into excellence. Excellence is not necessarily a quest for the unrealistic or impossible.

Deanna is in the midst of a wonderful project, a creative

process of developing an organic chocolate superfood to be sold in the marketplace, and also to be used as a teaching tool to advance awareness of the importance of healthy natural food to fuel the body. She hit a place in her process where she felt blocked and frustrated. She said to me at a time of confusion and annoyance, "I don't know what to do. I don't have a clue what to do next. I have hit a block." I said, "Congratulations! You are on the creative edge. Don't look at this as a block. Think of it as a part of the evolutionary path that takes normal and necessary turns on the journey to your destination. Mistakes are important in any creative process. Compare this to a baby learning to walk. The baby must fall and get up over and over again in order to strengthen and develop her muscles and gain the control needed for walking. Pat yourself on the back for your willingness to do whatever it takes to choose joy on your journey." Deanna went back to work with a smile on her face.

Stop focusing on the one pebble in your bowl of diamonds.

GROWTH EXERCISE
What Are Your Priorities?

It's important to learn to relax and be easier on yourself. There's a time to call it a day and turn off the computer and TV. Simply allow yourself to experience the beauty that exists in each moment. This is also an opportunity to get in touch with what your soul needs at its deepest level, to feel fully alive.

Remember, time is a gift. How you use it determines your experience of life. How are you using your time today? To help you reflect on this, start a new journal and answer these questions as they flow from your soul:

1. If today were the last day of your life, how were your activities important up until now? How important are the things you are still planning to do?

2. Which activities are essential in your life and which ones are not?

3. What needs to be done right away and what can be delayed without creating problems?

4. What activities do you value that need more of your time and effort, and what things do not?

Having a healthy, productive life is like riding a bicycle. If you keep worrying about having the perfect bike, gear, and weather, then you may never get going.

Take time today to make space to listen to your heart and find that small inner voice asking you to feed your soul with a beach walk, a warm bath, or time in the garden.

CLEARING YOUR POSSESSIONS

Duane Elgin, the author of *Voluntary Simplicity: Toward a Way of Life That Is Outwardly Simple, Inwardly Rich,* spoke at our spiritual center. His wonderful book, first published in 1981 and more recently revised, is a classic green treatise on liberating yourself from the pursuit of status symbols and living in balance to curtail the environmental consequences of mass consumption.

Duane sees us living in a consumer society that often operates under the pretense that more is better. This point of view places us under pressure to keep up with the Joneses. Unfortunately, when we think that way, we never arrive at where we want to go. Feeling incomplete always drives us to want something more. The first step out of this unhealthy pattern is being grateful for what we already have.

Duane also talked about living simply as *conscious consumers,* rather than out of a market-driven feeling that we *should* be buying something. For instance, being a conscious consumer could include asking, "Do I really need this?" when you have the impulse to buy. Try it! You'll be amazed how many times you really don't *need* an item; you just want it. Making that purchase could be a way to fill an emotional void. Being conscious also includes reusing items when you can. For example, my family has switched to cloth napkins and we recycle. Bottom line: How much you use does have an impact because our planet's natural resources are not limitless.

Becoming more conscious helps you tackle the clearing of your physical space. Do you see all the clutter? And how many times do you hang onto things just because you don't want to let them go? Meanwhile, those items clutter your space and make your living area less comfortable and more stressful.

My friend, Rebecca, was having her kitchen renovated, so she moved a lot of items into the garage. Among them was a large framed photo of a Santa Fe sunset, a gift from a dear friend she had lost touch with. When a neighbor asked if she could have it, Rebecca resisted at first. Her neighbor had always been helpful, and Rebecca saw that giving the woman the framed photo could be a small gesture of appreciation. After the neighbor picked up the framed photo, Rebecca looked in her garage and smiled. The neighbor had actually given her a gift too—one less item to clear away!

Look around your living space with conscious eyes. How many things do you no longer need? Could you move any of the items elsewhere in your home and use them in a new way? Do you know someone else who could use one or more of them? Is there a thrift store or other charity that would appreciate receiving some of these things? As you begin to clear your clutter, notice how it helps you feel more centered and less scattered.

A Question for Conscious Consumers:
What do I truly need in this moment to stay in
alignment with my purpose?

ASSESSING YOUR RELATIONSHIPS

In the last chapter, we explored the importance of being around positive people. One crucial aspect of awareness is noticing who we're spending time with. In addition to choosing to be around uplifting people, it's necessary to take a periodic inventory and let go of relationships that don't really fit well into our lives. Perhaps your values have changed and you have less in common with a friend who still sees things in an old way. Or maybe you've been putting a lot of energy into trying to change someone to fit into your life, when you really need to be doing the work of *changing yourself* to fit your life. Instead of giving yourself wings, you may have attached yourself to someone who drags you down.

GREEN GROWTH STRATEGY

Everyone comes into your life for a reason. That doesn't mean they're meant to be there *always*. There are appropriate times to release relationships. At the same time, some relationships need to be worked on. Don't have a policy of considering relationships as disposable. Interestingly, sometimes all we need to do to improve a relationship is to unhook ourselves from an expectation; this can free up the relationship for growth and a different and deeper connection. In these cases, there's still meaning in the relationship but it's been bound up in expectations that the person can never meet.

Weighing the choices of keeping a relationship or letting it go is a heartfelt process. Some healthy green questions to ask during these times are:

Do I have anything more to give this relationship?

Is there anything else that I have to learn here?

I had to make hard choices about relationships around the time of my daughter's death. I searched for support for healing and a place to be inspired. I decided to attend a meeting of a group of parents who had lost a child. It didn't take long for me to realize that this wasn't the right place for my recovery. There were people in that grieving circle who had been attending for fifteen years. I knew that these long-term members hadn't worked through their pain.

One day, I stood up and told the group, "I know this isn't a place Tara would want me to be. I plan to heal." I left and never returned. I wouldn't have made such comments before Tara's death, but along with my pain and grief had come the intention to do whatever it would take to heal my heart. My willingness and determination to let go of being stuck in grief soon led me to a spiritual teacher and others who helped me reach a place of greater understanding and purpose and to cultivate more joy.

It's imperative to have a group of people available to share the wide variety of events in our lives; however, we need to make wise choices. What we don't want is to be with anyone who sits around and complains. We need a safe place to enjoy ongoing spiritual renewal and a sense of support and community.

When one door closes, another one opens,
but we so often look so long and so regretfully upon the closed
door that we do not see the ones which open for us.
ALEXANDER GRAHAM BELL

☐

Here is an inspirational prayer to help you let go of your fear of change and everything else you need to release. How do you let go? You let go by surrendering.

Prayer of Surrender

Today I surrender all my fears and uncertainty to Spirit.
I confidently move forward with faith and love.
I know that there is One Intelligence from which everything is made.
Spirit, that created the wonders of the Universe, certainly knows
how to direct and guide me in my divine purpose.
I clearly focus on my intention to evolve and expand my Divine Nature.

As I surrender my need to know and my need to control,
I become a co-creator with the Universe.
I turn my thoughts away from troubles, difficulties and problems
to focus on a greater good that is waiting to be revealed.
I see the possibility in all situations.
I recognize that all life is infused with the wisdom and creative essence of Spirit.

As I surrender to the expansiveness of Spirit, I am filled with Trust and Gratitude.
I am grateful for the awareness
that there is a power for Good ever available for me to use.
I know that with God all things are possible.
Filled with peace and possibility, I move confidently out into my day
knowing I am never alone.
I am ever grateful! And so it is.

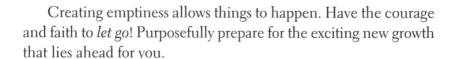

Creating emptiness allows things to happen. Have the courage and faith to *let go*! Purposefully prepare for the exciting new growth that lies ahead for you.

WHAT'S NEXT?

Sometimes you need to release the sad stories about your lifetime's woe. Obviously there's more to be gained from seeing these stories in a spiritual light than in allowing them to bring you down. Chapter 4 will help you continue the process of setting yourself free by letting go.

> Although the world is very full of suffering,
> it is also full of the overcoming of it.
>
> HELEN KELLER

☐

Preparing for New Growth

Awareness and Deep Listening to Life

Real wealth is ideas plus energy.

R. BUCKMINSTER FULLER

The higher your energy level,
the more efficient your body.
The more efficient your body,
the better you feel and
the more you will use your talent
to produce outstanding results.

ANTHONY ROBBINS

While it's important to create the space for living in your full potential, it's also critical to delve deeper in order to discover the resources and blocks within you. In life, we must have the energy to fuel our dreams and visions. In nature, an acorn will not grow into an oak tree unless it has enough sunlight, water, air, and soil nutrients. Though the ground in a garden may look fine, the underlying conditions in the earth might include clay soil, rocks, acidity, and more bad stuff. In life, underlying conditions might be unresolved hurts and confusion left by past experiences and painful memories that block your available energy to manifest your vision.

In the last chapter, you began the work of greening your life for the changes ahead. Now it is time to be conscious of the energy you put into something, the source of that energy, and how efficiently that energy is used. Today, the world is facing an energy crisis because it runs on finite resources. We are looking to nature to find renewable sources of energy. Sunlight, wind, and water are renewable energies that can provide us with fuel for transportation and electricity.

Where do you get the energy to live your best life? Do you get it from your ego's finite and temporal successes and failures? Or do you get your energy from connecting to your highest self, which is always unlimited and renewable?

Reuseable Energy

Renewable energy effectively uses natural resources such as sunlight, wind, rain, tides, and geothermal heat, which are naturally replenished. Renewable energy technologies range from solar power, wind power, hydroelectricity/micro hydro, biomass and biofuels for transportation. On the other hand, an energy crisis is any great bottleneck (or price increase) in the supply of energy resources to an economy. It usually refers to the shortage of oil and additionally to electricity or other natural resources. An energy crisis may be referred to as an oil crisis, petroleum crisis, energy shortage, electricity shortage, or electricity crisis.

You have a choice. Either you choose to live in denial of your deeper issues, and thwart your ability to be green, or delve into your dark places and bring light to them. Bringing light means gaining a higher perspective about your past so you can live with a deeper spiritual understanding.

Surface spirituality which demands you always act happy despite your unresolved issues just doesn't cut it. Without being addressed, the old issues might cause you to act in ways that lead to self-sabotage. Plus, when you wear only rose-colored glasses, you deny the sad and painful parts of life which are real aspects of your existence and the food for learning and growth.

The gains that come from this work are twofold. First, there's insight regarding potential for your growth. Second, you discover the lessons your past experiences can make available to you. So, take a deep breath, remain open to the idea of healing, and continue moving forward.

WHERE ARE YOU PUTTING YOUR ENERGY?

Sometimes you navigate life on automatic pilot, never noticing how you are wasting energy on dead issues. If you're remembering your mother ignoring you when you were seven, or a sweetheart dumping you in high school, or a boss mistreating you in a former job, then you're funneling energy into issues that no longer serve you. This energy drain can be debilitating. You could be directing energy toward planting new thoughts and growing new possibilities. You could be devoting it to improving your present conditions as well as your future.

Until you are willing to go deep inside and unhook your trapped energy, you can't be fully in the flow of creative possibilities in the Universe. It's helpful to jot down two lists to make yourself more aware of where your energy is focused. The first list looks at where your energy has been directed lately. The second list helps to refocus on your goals.

| **GROWTH EXERCISE** |

Energy Patterns

Take out your journal now and work with the following questions:

Current/Past Energy Patterns

1. Where am I putting my energy right now?
2. Is my energy going toward reliving old experiences that I really don't want anymore?
3. What dead issues are draining my energy?
4. Are there areas taking up my energy that do not serve the highest and best possibility for my life?
5. What issues are draining my energy that could be used in more positive ways?

The Conscious Direction of Your Energy

1. Where do I want to focus my energy?
2. What steps could I be taking now to support my growth?
3. What areas of my life need development?
4. What parts of myself have I been neglecting?
5. What aspects of my life are calling out for support?

Once you have addressed both categories of questions, review your responses and create an energy priority list. Make a list of the ten most positive priorities for your future that deserve your energy. Then consider your responses to the questions in the first section and identify the major issues that have been holding your energy hostage. Use the ideas in this chapter to clear the old issues so your energy is freed up to build your new life.

It's important to use your priority list as motivation for clearing the deeper issues. It's essential to ground yourself in your previously stated positive direction as you do this difficult work. Otherwise, you run the risk of being pulled into despair. Keep your positive desires for growth and new possibilities close to your heart as you work through this exercise.

> Dwell as near as possible
> to the channels
> in which life flows.
> HENRY DAVID THOREAU

☐

Personal Energy

Here's another reason to clear out the negativity left behind from your past experiences. The quality of your personal energy has a function in the Universe; it draws experiences that have a similar energy to what you're putting out, like a magnet. Because 10 percent of our energy comes from the conscious mind, and 90 percent comes from the unconscious, it's wise to purge the unpleasant negative internal energy periodically. That way, you have a rich, vibrant, positive energy field in which to grow your potential.

> Your pain is the breaking of the shell
> that encloses your understanding.
> KAHLIL GIBRAN

☐

BREAKING APART VS. CRACKING OPEN

When life deals you tragedies or hardships, your heart breaks. You may try using putty to cover the cracks and then attempt to proceed as if nothing has occurred. But if you allow the crack to break open, your heart may actually grow bigger with more love, passion, and understanding. How does this happen? *By doing the work of healing your many wounds.* When we allow ourselves to crack open, things and situations that we haven't examined begin to surface.

In the days after Tara was taken in the car accident, I was in shock and couldn't understand why a horrible tragedy would occur in the lives of good people. I sought out my spiritual advisor and, through my sobs, told her how I was struggling with this question of *why*. She said I was not to know right then why it happened. And that if I *was* to know why, the answer would come later, at the right time. She added that if I insisted on holding onto the question of why, my choice would prevent me from healing.

I learned a powerful lesson: The initial step in healing is to let go of the need to know *why* something happened. Instead you must shift attention to these questions:

What's here for me to learn?
How am I meant to grow?

Interestingly, our bodies and spirits release pain in a progressive way. They know how to gradually surface our wounds for healing. After Tara left us, the Universe directed a series of different healers to me at appropriate times. My body and mind were in pain and shock.

A beautiful woman and gifted healer appeared in my life and offered me her gift of healing. She would spend hours with me not just as a massage therapist, relieving my physical aches and pains, but also as an emotional healer moving me not only through the great pain of the loss of a child, but also the pains that were revealed from my childhood—molestation and unworthiness. She moved me along my healing process as I was ready.

One morning I awoke suddenly to realize I'd just been released from a state of shock. Suddenly the hole I had felt in my solar plexus was gone.

During the previous sixteen months, I had not been forced to deal with the totality of my loss all at once. I learned that we must trust the process of healing, pace ourselves, and know that the wisdom of our bodies and spirits will be pacing our progress as well.

> A real voyage of discovery
> exists not in seeing new landscapes
> but in having new eyes.
> MARCEL PROUST

☐

GROWTH EXERCISE
Reveal, Heal and Transform Your Baggage

To complete this exercise, some tools are required. You'll need:

- A cloth handbag with a lengthy attached strap, or a drawstring bag with long cording. The strap or cording should be long enough to allow the bag to hang down loosely from your neck to around the area of your heart.

- Some small stones or pebbles—either ones that you've gathered yourself, or the polished and washed type that are used for finishing off a planter box.

- The cloth bag will be used to hold the stones. The bag should be able to hold an amount of stones heavy enough for you to feel their weight comfortably against the back of your neck as the purse hangs down.

With your tools in hand, go to a quiet place where you'll have privacy and won't be interrupted. To begin, sit in a relaxed manner and get in touch with your higher self. Next, put the stones inside the bag, blessing them with the intention of understanding their meaning to you. Then place the strap or cording around the back of your neck and pull the bag down near your heart. As you allow the bag to hang near your heart, ask yourself, What is the major issue of baggage from my past that is blocking me from all the joy and good in the world?

Now feel the weight of the stones pressing against the back of your neck and see what thoughts come up for you. What pain have you been carrying around? This exercise is helpful because it will assist you in identifying the hurts and wounds from your past that need to be addressed. You can't heal an issue unless it has been revealed to you.

Allow a situation related to your issues to come into your consciousness. See what surfaces and who's involved. Bring an awareness of the essence of the other person into your consciousness. Be with them. Now tell the other person how you feel. Really let out everything that has been bothering you. Get it out of your system. Be very honest about it. For example, if you feel like you invested time and energy in a relationship that was a dead end for you, you might say:

I am really hurt that you didn't look out for my interests in having a long-term relationship.

I am upset that you misrepresented yourself as someone who could be that for me.

I am angry about how little you gave for all that I was willing to give to you.

I am mad that you weren't more careful about working on issues in a way that would make things work for us.

Once you've let it all out, imagine this person giving you their perspective on the situation. Tell them that you'd like to know what was going on in their life at that time. What was it like for them to experience what happened? Ask the Universe to allow a greater understanding to be revealed to you.

The two of you can continue to have more turns talking. Visualize the exchange until you feel the conversation is complete.

Now take the situation out of the status of being a problem into the realm of possibility and healing. Remind yourself that we are here to make progress, not to be perfect. Then ask yourself:

What lessons does this situation have to offer me?
How have I grown from this?
What more is there to learn?
Did I represent myself clearly and honestly?

What are the possible lessons? If it's about a love relationship, are you focusing on the wrong types of qualities in a partner? If it's about business dealings, do you need to be more astute about the people you work with? If it's a health issue, your lessons could be learning that you are much more than your body, that you need to slow down and take better care of yourself, that you can focus on something besides your physical pain or discomfort, or that life is short and our time here is precious.

After you've figured out what there is to learn from the situation, ask yourself this important question:

What inner gift must I remember in order to let this situation go?

If you made a poor choice in a relationship partner, remember that you have the power to make a better choice at any time. If it's a financial difficulty, remember that you are a creative being, capable of creating abundance in your life. If it's a creative challenge, bring to mind all the creative things you've done in your life and affirm that you can learn from your mistakes.

Once you've been able to gain a higher perspective on the situation and have grasped its lesson, there is one final step. Tell yourself:

I release this situation and I release this person with love and understanding.

I appreciate and remain open to any new learning.

Thank you, Universe, for this new understanding.

Now it's time to end this session. You can remove the bag from around your neck and go on with your day. Feel good about your work in reframing this experience and gleaning the good it has to offer you. Revisit the exercise whenever you can, to continually clear out the dead issues from your past.

The beauty of this exercise is that it quickly brings old issues into your awareness. Because we hold onto issues physically in our bodies, we sometimes need to use physical methods to get in touch with them. This exercise is simple, and it works.

> Hanging onto resentment
> is like taking poison
> and waiting for the other person to die.
> MALACHY MCCOURT

☐

THE HEALING CHOICE OF FORGIVENESS

As Malachy McCourt's quote reveals, when we fail to forgive someone, we usually hurt ourselves. Many times, the other person doesn't even realize that we still resent what they did. Meanwhile the pain is ours.

Forgiveness is the one thing we can do to heal our lives and relationships—the healing antidote for just about every situation. Still, it may be difficult to forgive. You may feel you deserve to be treated better. Yet an essential part of forgiveness is realizing that it doesn't mean that you're condoning the other person's behavior or giving them permission to act that way again. You're simply choosing not to hang onto the resentment any longer. You realize that people do the best they can at any particular moment.

As a part of letting go of the hurts of the past, I suggest you create a list of everyone you need to forgive. Some of the people you want to forgive will be obvious and others less so. One clue that there's a need for forgiveness is when you keep running a situation over and over again in your mind. You just can't seem to let it go.

Another indicator is when you've become more withdrawn from the person, a situation, or life in general. Maybe you've completely shut down in that area. Or perhaps you can recall having a big reaction to the person's behavior when the incident occurred. Once you've created a list of people to forgive, prioritize the names based on those situations which are draining your energy the most.

Next, write letters to the people, starting at the top of the list. In each letter, express the depth of your feelings, from sadness to frustration, to rage and even hatred. Just release all of the darkness that you're holding inside regarding this person. Some jumpstart phrases in your letter might be:

I am disappointed because...

I'm hurt because...

I feel angry because...

As you write each letter, tune into your body and keep expressing your thoughts until it feels like your pain has been purged. Once you've cleared the hurt, you can either burn the letter or tear it up into little pieces. As you burn the letter and scatter the ashes, or as you rip it up, repeat the words:

Today I release my resentment toward [name]. I forgive [him/her], and bless [him/her], as I let go of the experience and refocus on things that bring joy, love and possibility into my life.

No matter how horrific a situation is that calls for forgiveness, it offers an opportunity to increase your compassion and understanding. Sometimes you have no idea of the amount of pain that another person is in, how emotionally wounded their hearts are. I once read a story of a woman who found enough compassion in her heart to reach out to the murderer who had killed her daughter. The woman developed a relationship with the man, who was then in prison, to see how she could help him. That is ultimate forgiveness.

While you're thinking about those you need to forgive, don't forget about yourself. In those situations where you need to forgive yourself, realize that you also did the best you could. Look for the lessons and make a commitment to your growth in these areas. Ask yourself, "What do I need to learn from this?" Forgiving yourself is as essential as forgiving others, if not more crucial.

Forgiveness is a daily practice.
LOUISE HAY

□

GROWTH EXERCISE

Setting Things Right—An Evening Practice

Often at the end of the day, you may feel something needs to be set right. You may be left with a vague sense of uneasiness, or know exactly what it is that's bothering you. Perhaps you spoke harshly to someone, treated a person without respect, made a mistake that affected another person, or didn't deliver on a commitment. Instead of berating yourself as the hours of the day dwindle, make it a practice to note what needs to be set right.

I do this every night, and it's a beautiful way to end the day. In my mind before going to sleep, I ask myself if there is anything related to the day's activities that I need to put back into alignment with good. Was there anywhere that I went off track since the previous bedtime? Then I ask myself if there's any action I need to take the following day. Does the situation require an apology? Do I need to bless this person and let it go? Do I need to make amends in some way?

The "Setting Things Right" practice is purifying. It lets you use your energy to make things good in your life. It's a great approach for avoiding getting caught up in the drama of the day and instead creating feelings of contentment about your involvement with the world. You'll sleep more peacefully, feel happier, and experience less guilt.

Of course, we always bless the good we experience, but this way we can also deal with the difficulties that arise. This practice helps you become the light that helps to heal the world.

> If we have no peace,
> it's because we've forgotten
> that we belong to each other.
> MOTHER THERESA

☐

GETTING HELP, GIVING HELP

We all have talents and gifts to share with the world; but we can't do everything alone. As you work through your old hurts, it's beneficial to seek help from those who can assist you as well as to offer your skills to others. I'm closing this chapter with some thoughts on getting support in the areas where you need it, and being of service where you can make a contribution.

As you work on personal growth and spirituality, it's essential to ask yourself: *Is this work that I can do by myself, or is this an area that I need help facilitating?* At the same time, you can express your intention with a silent request using phrasing such as: *Spirit, guide me to those I need to be with at this time.* Then allow the Universe to direct you to the right people.

There are so many different types of people who can assist you with your growth—spiritual counselors, psychologists, breath work coaches, bodyworkers, women's support groups, men's support groups, coed support groups, classes, workshops, and more. Be in touch with the energy of the situation and see what assistance pulls at you energetically. Choose the options that feel safe.

Sometimes help comes in the form of a good friend. Such a friend may be in tune with you and reach out to pull you back into the light when you're feeling down. Summon the courage to share your darker feelings with them by bringing up the issue you're struggling with. Often, a good friend can help you view your situation from a higher perspective, and assist you in recognizing the many resources you have available. Such a true friend is a great gift and someone you'll want to honor by being there for them in a similar way when they need you.

What about being of service during the more difficult periods of our lives? Giving of yourself and your time can make you realize that others are struggling with similar issues, and/or reinforce your awareness that you can make a positive impact on the world. Your service may take the simple form of bringing kindness and compassion to your workplace. Or you may take on an independent service project that taps into your specific skills. You might volunteer your time in a group effort related to an issue that deeply touches your heart. When you note the issues that really get your goat, you will realize where you're called to serve.

Remember This: Working on yourself helps you to change the energetic qualities of the Universe. When you reach out for help or to be of help, you spread your higher energies out into the world which also needs a great deal of healing.

> Peace on the outside
> comes from peace on the inside;
> Peace on the inside comes from understanding
> that we are one with God.
> SHIRLEY MACLAINE

□

WHAT'S NEXT?

Life unfolds like a flower. Each flower has a unique design and beauty to reveal. Within each of us there is Divine Plan waiting to be discovered and expressed. It is revealed to us in evolving visions, each growing out of the previous one. So what's the next step? *Visioning*—creating a vision of what your life would look like if you allowed it to grow into its potential magnificence. Visioning is a fun, exciting, and vital action toward harvesting your dreams.

> It takes only 16 seconds
> to begin a manifestation.
> LYNN GRABHORN

□

CHAPTER 5

Creating a Vision

Using Renewable Energy by Tapping into Source

Your vision will become clear
only when you look into your heart.

Who looks outside, dreams.
Who looks inside, awakens.

CARL JUNG

The more you lose yourself in something bigger than yourself,
the more energy you will have.

NORMAN VINCENT PEALE

Imagine we are born of a universal intelligence and within each of us is a creative pattern for life. Often we make the mistake of looking outside ourselves to find this creative pattern. In order for your pattern to be revealed, you must take some valuable time to deeply listen. This kind of listening requires patience, practice, and perseverance. You must be totally committed to do whatever it takes to connect with and reveal your vision. Sometimes this requires letting go of something— or everything—and often it requires intense focus.

Visioning

Reverend Dr. Michael Bernard Beckwith says that **VISIONING** is a process by which we train ourselves to be able to hear, feel, see, and catch God's plan for our life or for any particular project we may be working on. Visioning is an organic process that evolves as one grows spiritually and is based on the idea that we're not here to tell God what to do or ask God for things, but to absolutely be available for what God is doing now and to open up to catch what's already happening.

One reason why the earth is in peril is our inability or unwillingness to listen to her divine plan. We have the mentality and practice of conquering and controlling, based on how we think things should be, passing judgment and placing artificial value on the sacred. The earth knows how to cultivate a forest. There are distinct and successive steps involved. Nature is patient and allows the forest to evolve into a complex, high-functioning, highly diverse and strong system.

Why can't we be like nature? Why do we become impatient, confused, and dissatisfied with the beautiful gift of life? We are uncertain about how to reveal our inherent gifts, so we often look outside of ourselves instead of listening to our deep inner wisdom. We must commit to understanding the subtle energies within that guide and direct us to our next evolutionary step. Listen!

The reason you and I become confused and dissatisfied with the beautiful gift of life lies in our uncertainty about how to reveal our own inherent gifts. We look outside of ourselves instead of listening to the deep wisdom and knowing that comes from inside. We know better.

If you are living in self-imposed chains, you will find the key to unlocking them when you discover the greater vision for your life. In this chapter, you will learn about the exciting and motivating process known as *visioning*.

THE PARALYSIS OF INDECISION

At six feet four inches with striking good looks, the late Christopher Reeve presented the perfect image of Superman on the movie screen. Though his acting background and interests also included stage appearances, such as in the Broadway production A *Matter of Gravity* co-starring Katharine Hepburn, it was his role as the superhero from the planet Krypton that catapulted Reeve to international acclaim as an actor. He brought a powerful intent to his role. "What makes Superman a hero is not that he has power, but that he has the wisdom and the maturity to use the power wisely," Reeve said. "From the acting point of view, that's how I approached the part." This statement would foreshadow how Reeve would choose to approach his own life when it later took an unexpected and challenging turn.

It seemed the ultimate irony when Reeve, our Superman, was physically paralyzed in an accident in 1995 while pursuing his off-screen passion—horseback riding. Yet in the soul-searching time that followed the injury, Reeve realized that the greatest paralysis a person could suffer was the paralysis of indecision. Despite his disability, he decided to use his power and influence in the world to make a difference. Unbelievably, Christopher Reeve remained our Superman by becoming an advocate of treatments and cures for paralysis stemming from spinal cord injuries and other nervous system disorders.

You can be afraid to decide what you want from life, but *only when you have the courage to claim, speak, and own your vision will it manifest.* Even when confronted with paralysis, Christopher Reeve found the inner strength to find a vision for his life that would give it purpose and passion. He showed us that our courage can allow us to fly and that the human spirit can soar, no matter what our circumstances.

When you try to hold on to things the way they are, you prevent something greater from emerging. A vision gives you something to stretch into so you can break the confines of normalcy and do something extraordinary. Sometimes a tragedy opens you up to new possibilities. Better yet, you take stock before tragedy hits by responding to a rumbling discontent in your heart and envisioning the changes that you want to make before it's too late.

> So many of our dreams at first seem impossible,
> then they seem improbable, and then,
> when we summon the will, they soon
> become inevitable.
> CHRISTOPHER REEVE

□

OUR VISION: A PERSONAL NAVIGATION SYSTEM

Today's cars often come with a global positioning and navigation system to help drivers make their way to destinations. The workings of these systems can be compared to how our vision operates in the Universe. For instance, before either the car's navigation system or our vision can work, a couple of steps must be taken.

Step 1.
Car: You need to turn on the ignition before the navigating system will operate.
You: You must turn on your awareness and set your general intention before you vision.

Step 2.

Car: You must tell the navigation system where you want to go, and then go there.

You: Your vision tells the Universe where you are headed.

Would you ever enter, "Oh, I don't care, take me anywhere" into a car's navigation system? Probably not, because you could find yourself driving around in circles. In the same way, if you want to avoid going round and round in unproductive patterns in your life, you must let the Universe know where you're headed by embracing and proclaiming your vision. In other words, *you must have your destination in mind.*

Informing these systems—the automated car navigation *and* the Universe—of your chosen destination activates them to work for you. Once you receive their messages, you can choose to follow the directives—or not.

With the car's navigation system, you may recall that a road along its suggested route currently is undergoing reconstruction. So you might choose different streets for that leg of your journey. In the same way, just as the Universe sends you messages throughout the day to support your vision, you can choose the best ways to respond to them. The messages may arrive through songs on the radio, conversations with friends, colleagues or strangers, articles you notice in magazines and newspapers, and so forth.

I continually keep my spiritual antennas up for messages being revealed in my life. Spirit speaks in so many creative ways. One of my favorite songs in high school was, and still is, "Do You Believe in Magic" by The Lovin' Spoonful. It never ceases to amaze me how that song will play on the radio when I am looking for confirmation about a certain issue. People are always synchronously speaking to me about things, unbeknownst to them, that answer a question I am holding in my heart. I love how life responds in such creative ways to guide me on the path to manifesting my dreams.

Upon receiving each message from the Universe, you'll want to tune into your intuition or inner knowing and see whether or not it fits. Dr. Wayne Dyer suggests that you ask yourself the following question when you seek guidance from your inner knowing: "Will this bring me peace of mind or not?" Usually when trying on something that doesn't fit, you feel uncomfortable—a signal that it isn't right for you. If it feels right, you then decide the best ways to respond.

Remember This: Visioning is not day planning.
It's what you see long-term for your future.

VISIONING 101

For a plant to grow, it needs the right nutrients and good soil. In the same way, to allow your vision to rise up from your inner awareness and expand into knowingness, you'll want to surround yourself in a field of healthy positive energy. To do the visioning work, it's helpful to create a sacred space somewhere in your environment that can support good energy. This might be a section of a particular room where there is a comfortable chair or recliner. You could clear the clutter from this indoor space, and then decorate it with posters that have spiritual themes and brightly colored accessories.

Alternately, you might select a serene outdoor area on your property that has a bench or a grassy spot where you could sit or recline on a blanket. You could embellish the outdoor space with such things as a statue of a smiling Buddha and a colorful wind catcher. You might also switch back and forth between two such spaces. In any case, it's important to have a quiet and peaceful space where you won't be interrupted.

My home is filled with sacred spaces. My living room has a comfy chair that I love to sit in, many green plants, and pieces of antique furniture with great memories. This space offers me great peace and comfort. I have a space in my office that has green plants, candles, books, and articles from my travels (Tibetan singing bowls, African art, Native American drums) as well as a wonderful poster that says: "It'll cost nothing to DREAM and everything not to." This space gives me inspiration. My bedroom is dark with a fireplace and two cozy chairs. This room offers me clarity and depth.

As you relax in your sacred space, take a deep breath and allow yourself to fill up with the knowledge that you live in a Creative Universe that loves and supports you. Release any thoughts of doubt or fear, noting them and then letting them go. Just fill yourself up with thoughts of God's love. Continue to breathe deeply. Let yourself feel safe, clear, and radiant, enveloped by the love of the Universe.

Next, open your heart and mind to receive Divine messages. To bring them forth, meditate on the following questions:

What is the greatest expression of my life that is trying to grow right now?

What is it that I am becoming?

After this beginning, you'll want to further prompt the visioning process. Over the years, I've developed a number of ways of optimizing this process. In addition to the basic questions above, here's your first additional vision optimizer. Optimizer questions are helpful if no messages about your vision come from the starter questions. They're also good to simply spur you to go deeper. I call this technique "Looking back at yourself as you were in your childhood." Ask yourself these questions:

What did I enjoy as a child?

What brought me fulfillment during those childhood years?

What talents did I allow to shine through in my childhood?

Another method of fertilizing your vision is to keep asking yourself the question, *Who am I?* Keep doing this for perhaps five minutes. Here are some answers that would be typical for me.

Q: Who am I?
A: I'm a woman.

Q: Who am I?
A: I'm a mother, wife, minister, teacher, author, and much more.

Eventually you can get really deep into the question of "Who am I?" At that point, try prompting yourself by finishing the phrase:

I am a being on this planet who is here to make a difference in the world by…

Some of my answers have been… *writing, speaking, art, singing and through personal connection.* See what rings true for you. By the way, you may wonder how I know that you're here to make a difference. It's because I believe that's true for everyone.

A strong vision is bigger than you are.
It's not something that necessarily fits right now.
It will make you stretchhhhhhhhhhhhhhhhhhhhhhhhhh!

MOVING PAST RESISTANCE THROUGH THE DARK EMOTIONS

If a vision is something you will grow into, how do you believe in your dream? If the idea is to create a joyous vision of something that's not you quite yet, how do you stay open to recognizing it?

Earlier in the book, you read about the ego and how it wants to keep you the same so you'll always know what to do. The ego wants to keep you from blooming. One way to empower yourself is to move out of ego thinking and into your Higher Self. Unlike the ego, the Higher Self wants to live in harmony and in co-creation with Spirit.

Sometimes when we resist acknowledging our vision, we can be stuck in the ego and in one of the darker emotions, such as jealousy, anger, or fear. By taking a closer look at what you are experiencing emotionally, you may find that your vision will then start to surface. To that end, try the following powerful exercise—another fertilizer for the vision.

GROWTH EXERCISE
Examine Dark Emotions

While sitting in your sacred space, take a deep breath and reflect on your life today. See what difficult emotion you're experiencing related to your future. Is it fear, jealousy, or anger? Once you've identified the emotion, write down a line in your journal to represent the strongest incident involving it. Here's an example that a friend shared with me.

Emotion: Jealousy

Incident: Recent lecture at my local health food store.

Now write down what you were jealous of:

I was jealous of the professional practice that the speaker had developed.

Realize that beneath your jealousy or anger is fear. Or if your original emotion was fear, under it will be more fear. Next, think about what you might be afraid of and write it down.

My fear is that I will never be able to leave my accounting job to become a health professional.

Hiding under your fear is what you truly want. Through examining your darker emotions, you can find the beauty of what your heart desires. The truth is that in the compost of life—those experiences involving tough emotions like jealousy—beauty can be found. This is a part of seeing everything in your life as a potential for growth.

LEARNING LESSONS FROM OUR ANGELS

Often we learn our greatest lessons from friends who see the truth when we cannot. Kirk and I met Jenny when we were presenting a workshop at Claremont College shortly after the release of Kirk's book, *Tara's Angels*. The workshop was about finding gifts and blessings in the challenges and tragedies of our lives. A large family of beautiful sisters in the class was dealing with their mother's recent diagnosis of breast cancer. The oldest sister, Jenny, was an angel herself, and we had an immediate connection.

Jenny loved the workshop and decided to make the ninety-minute drive from her home in Wrightwood to our store in San Juan Capistrano for weekly classes. She encouraged me to continue to share Tara's message of love and healing with a wider audience. She believed in me and encouraged me to grow. She was there every step of the way when we opened our Spiritual Center. She helped open the Center, from painting to planning, and continues to be there week in and week out. I know Spirit guides her messages and we have a bond that is much deeper than this physical experience. Jenny has been, and always will be, an angel in my life, gently inviting me to expand my horizons and live a life that is eternally green.

THE CHIEF AND HIS GRANDSON

One brisk summer night, an old Gabrielino Indian chief was sitting by a campfire with his young grandson. The two had been quiet for a while, watching the dancing flames from their perch on a long-fallen tree trunk. Off in the distance, crickets were chirping in the grasses and a whippoorwill chortled from high in a coastal live oak tree. Finally the chief said to the boy, "Inside of me, there is a horrible fight going on."

"Who's fighting?" his grandson replied.

"Two wolves," the chief answered.

"Why are they fighting?" the boy wanted to know.

"Because they are so different. One of the wolves is mean-spirited and cruel. He is hate, and intolerance, and deceit, and greediness. The other wolf is kind and good. He is loving, generous, forgiving, and fair. The second wolf has foresight and tremendous vision."

"Why is this fight inside *you*?" the boy wondered, looking at his grandfather with a puzzled expression.

"It is in me because it is in every human being, you included," the chief explained, watching his grandson with kind eyes.

"Grandfather, tell me, which wolf wins?" his grandson asked, wide-eyed in alarm.

"The one you feed," the chief answered with a gentle smile.

GROWTH EXERCISE

Tuning into Tree Wisdom

I mentioned earlier that I traveled with Brother Ishmael Tetteh and a group to Ghana, along the western coast of Africa. One of the places on our spiritual tour was the Aburi Botanical Gardens, located about an hour's drive from the city of Accra in the mountains. After we passed through the grassy areas in front of the Gardens where locals were drumming, we discovered a wide variety of trees among the exotic plant life—trees gathered from all over the world. Aburi was the perfect spot for us to spend time communing with trees and deciphering their wisdom.

Spending time with trees reminds you that everyone is part of something bigger, and that there is a Universe out there supporting us. You can use the wonderful natural energy of trees to calm your thoughts and cleanse your mind, so you can be open to receive your vision. Getting in touch with nature through trees is centering and very helpful for filtering out all the mental distractions that come from your day.

How do you connect with these beautiful and awesome natural creations of the Universe? Try the following exercise, yet another vision fertilizing technique:

1. **Select a place with trees** that has good energy and an environment that is peaceful and quiet. It might be a forest, a community park, or even your own backyard.

2. **Once there, take deep, slow breaths as you walk**, to help you relax your mind and body. Draw in the warmth of the sun as you move, and fill your soul with loving energy. Sense that you are a part of the natural world.

3. **Notice if you can feel different types of energy** coming off different types of trees as you stroll around the area. Then see which tree calls out to you the most. Once you've determined this, walk toward the tree, and feel the subtleties of its energy. Take in its beauty.

4. **Lay your hands on the trunk of the tree.** See if you can feel its energy in your palms. Through your hands, send a sense of gratitude toward the tree for sharing its energy with you.

5. **Sit with your back leaning against the base of the tree.** Breathe slowly once again, and relax your mind and body even further. As you continue to enjoy the tree's energy, begin to dialog with it. Ask the tree questions like: *What is it that I should know about the vision wanting to grow in my life?* Refine your questions as the answers start to come.

6. **Continue to commune with the tree** as long as you'd like. If you wish, you can jot down notes in your journal.

7. **Stand up, face the tree, and give thanks.** It is important to acknowledge how the energy from the tree supports your visioning work. (You can even hug the tree if you like.)

When I was at the Aburi Gardens, this process was extremely powerful. There was something about being in that ancient land which took me deeply into a profound experience of oneness with the Universe. Back home, I have also turned to my friends, the trees, many times for their wise counsel in my visioning work and meditations.

The intelligence of a seed to grow into a flower may seem
miraculous to someone who doesn't know there is a Divine
plan for everything.

GROWTH EXERCISE

Creating a Vision Box

There is another optimizing method that you might think of as visioning inside the box. For this one, you might want to grab a French beret and a white smock as you'll be drawing on your inner artist to create a physical representation of your vision. Some artistic options include creating vision collages or vision drawings or paintings, but for now, you are going to focus on the fun exercise of creating a *vision box.*

I've enjoyed my vision box so much that I have hung onto it for many years. One advantage of a vision box is that it's more flexible to update than a collage or painting. The basic idea is to have a small box in which you place envelopes and objects. Inside the envelopes, you put images or words that represent different aspects of your vision as well as items that are symbols of your vision. Decorate the outside of your box with images, words, and quotations, too.

Inside my visioning box, I have:

- **A postcard from Hawaii**—because I like to travel and the Aloha State is one of my peaceful places.
- **A picture of a church**—representing my dream and goal of building a beautiful new church for our Center.
- **The cover of a book**—it was my dream when I created the box to write a book.
- **An envelope of stickers with positive sayings**—they are "Make your life beautiful," "Plant happiness in your heart," and "Take time to dream."
- **An envelope with pictures of women I admire**—these pictures are of women such as TV news anchors Diane Sawyer and Katie Couric.

On the outside of my box, I have:

- **A prayer of surrender**—it says that I trust in the power of the Universe to help deliver my dream.
- **Other images and words**—powerful words and pictures that represent my vision.

This technique doesn't take much time, and it's easy. Find a sturdy, attractive box and start collecting items, images, quotes, and words to put into it. Decide on some categories to use to label your envelopes. Cut out images, quotations, and words from magazines, other periodicals, or printed Internet pages. The items you store inside could come from just about anywhere. A glue stick can be used to fasten things to the outside.

Have fun as you let your vision come into visual focus.

Be like the bird
That, pausing in her flight
Alights a while on boughs too slight,
Feels them give way
Beneath her and yet sings,
Knowing that she hath wings.

VICTOR HUGO

□

WHAT YOU FEEL IS WHAT YOU GET

In order for your vision to take root and grow, you'll need to offer it a fertile field. One way to do this is to create a full body experience of what it would feel like to have achieved the vision. This step changes your physical energy and will help draw your vision to you out of all the possibilities in the Universe. Yes, to an important extent in this Universe, *what you feel will be what you get!*

To understand this process, think about the following. How do successful salespeople prepare to ask for the business and close the sale? Don't they conjure up feelings of self-assurance that the deal will come through? Then, during the transaction, their confidence can become contagious.

Because these dynamic salespeople believe in their pitch, their customers are more likely to buy into it too. Now picture the untalented salesperson. He undercuts his ability to make a sale with feelings of defeat and doubt even before the transaction takes place! His lack of confidence may make the customer wonder if this is the person to be buying from. This is a simplified illustration, of course, compared to visioning and the Universe. However, this example presents the basic idea of why it's important to get into the right feeling place.

To bring up the desired positive feelings associated with your vision, ask yourself, *What greater expression of me wants to grow and have joy in my life?* Then get into the physical sensations associated with the mental pictures. Other questions to start with could be: *What am I called to create?* or *What vision wants to grow in my life?* Follow those basic questions with:

- How does my vision feel?
- What scents and smells are associated with it?
- How does it taste?
- How does it sound?

As the answers come to you, allow your whole body to awaken to the vision.

Sometimes it can be helpful to jumpstart this process. How? By using a tool that will give you the feelings you're going for. For instance, you might listen to a motivational tape that would give you the excitement of having your vision. Or you could watch a movie that captures the feelings your vision would generate. Or a song sometimes does the trick.

However you bring up the feelings, stay with them as much as possible. For when you own your vision on the feeling level, the Universe will begin to help you manifest it in your life.

YOUR VISION/GOD'S TIMING

Your vision is ignited. You have launched it with passion and know it will come to be, thanks to the energy you are vibrating and the Law of Attraction. What you may not know is that it will manifest in God's time, which is not necessarily what you want right now.

Remember This: There is a circular pattern to life cycles. Sometimes these cycles are quick; other times they take a long time to complete.

Every year since Tara crossed over, I have discovered that she has given me gifts on her birthday. These are small gifts such as an unexpected burst of yellow roses blooming on a bush in our backyard where few buds had appeared in the past. For the milestone of her thirtieth birthday on June 7, 2007, Tara presented me with a magnificent gift. She made her transition when she was fifteen, so thirty years meant we had been blessed with fifteen years of Tara in physical form and fifteen years of her presence as our angel.

On the morning of Tara's thirtieth birthday, Peggy, a wonderful nurse practitioner and founder of the Center's Health Ministry, took me to a *Take Your Clergy to Work* breakfast at the hospital where she works. I arrived early and sat at a table with a nice man who introduced himself as the trauma chaplain. He told me about his connection with a local family who had recently lost three small children in a car accident. The pain of this tragedy affected the entire community and was still weighing heavily on my heart. I was touched by his commitment and ongoing involvement with the family. As I listened to him my mind traveled back fifteen years to this same hospital where Tara had been pronounced dead. There was no chaplain on duty when we heard the devastating news, and there was no one who could help us with the crushing blow of pain. I thought about how much better it could have been for us if someone like this man had been there for us.

I remembered calling the hospital several times during the weeks after our tragedy to tell them I didn't want any other family to experience what I had that night without support. I offered to be there to help—any time night or day. Although a call never came, seven years later while sharing our story at an interfaith breakfast, a woman chaplain came up to us afterwards and explained that because of the situation with our daughter and my pleas for family support in these cases, the hospital had implemented a 24-hour Trauma Chaplaincy program. Now, fifteen years later, on Tara's birthday, I suddenly realized how our story had come full circle.

This was Tara's gift to me that day. Knowing that a strong network of spiritual, physical, and emotional support had been there for the current family in need transported me into a feeling of deep gratitude and lightness in my heart. It was a wonderful example of how sometimes we plant seeds and nothing happens. But something can be happening beyond our realm of senses. The results may not become clear until weeks, months, or years later, when something appears and we feel that sense of joyful triumph.

> The breeze at dawn has secrets to tell you;
> Don't go back to sleep.
> You must ask for what you really want;
> Don't go back to sleep...
>
> RUMI

☐

WHAT'S NEXT?

As you focus on the vision of your life, your divine purpose will be revealed. Personal fulfillment, joy, and richness come when you clarify what your unique contribution is in life and are true to it. Because purpose is so crucial to having a satisfying and passionate life, Chapter 6 will help you reflect on this essential aspect of your vision.

> It's not enough to have lived.
> We should be determined
> to live for something.
> LEO F. BUSCAGLIA

☐

Refining Your Life's Design

Finding Your Niche – Living with Purpose

The place where God calls you to
is the place where your deep gladness
meets the world's needs.

FREDERICK BUECHNER

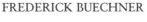

There is just one life for each of us:
our own.

EURIPIDES

Many people are concerned about whether there is life after
death. "What's going to happen to me afterwards?" they ask me.
"If my spirit lives on, what experiences will I have?" A more essential question is, "Am I really alive in my present life?" Are you set
on autopilot or are you living on purpose? Being aligned with your
purpose comes from knowing why you're here, this lifetime. What's
the unique gift that you bring to the world? As you create the vision
of your new life, make sure that your *purpose* is a major influence
on your life's design.

Being "on purpose" means participating fully in every minute
of your life—both the pleasant and the unpleasant ones—and
receiving the gifts they bring. In this chapter, you will identify and
fine-tune your sense of purpose.

Purpose: The Fabric of Your Life

Your purpose is Interwoven into the Fabric of Your Life. It's what you were created to be and do. If you look back at your life right now, you'll find that your purpose is what connects all of your experiences. Purpose is interwoven into everything.

Teaching has been the consistent thread interlaced through the experiences of my life — *my purpose*. I was never guided by my parents to become a teacher. However, there was an internal guidance system that directed me to go to the University of Southern California (USC) to major in English and get my teaching credential. And after college, I worked as an elementary school teacher for over twenty years. Even at the spiritual center today, my mission is to be part of a teaching ministry. Though my job title is no longer formally "teacher," I still am teaching.

What about my earlier life? One thing I remember from my childhood is that I was always playing school. Whether I was hanging out with my friends or my dolls, I played school and was the teacher.

In my teen years, I became very involved in my speech class and the debate team. And those activities were all related to the role of teaching, too. There was the preparation for the talks, the studying, and then the speaking. And my special gifts were recognized in high school when I won third prize in a speech tournament held at USC.

When I visited the USC campus for the tournament, I decided that's where I wanted to attend college. Once enrolled, I became very involved in my sorority, Alpha Delta Pi. At the sorority, my teaching took another form — pledge trainer. My role was to help new pledges adjust, get to know the group, and see how they could get involved in our activities. I taught them the ropes for succeeding at the sorority.

Once I graduated from USC, I went right into the teaching profession. I taught young children for sixteen years in the school system in Torrance, California, and then for another four years in Orange County. Eventually I got a masters in educational administration, not realizing that my new skills would be used in running a church, not a school.

What purpose is interwoven through the timeline of your life? Have you always loved to interact with children? Did your knack for number crunching stand out? Were you always taking charge and being the leader? Do you see that you were often performing in some way and entertaining others? What type of activity, natural gift, or spontaneous inclination seems to connect everything that you've done? Remember that your purpose probably fit itself into different roles through time, though its essence didn't change.

It is better to perform one's own duties imperfectly than to master the duties of another. By fulfilling the obligations he is born with, a person never comes to grief.

KRISHNA

□

A HINDU LEGEND: *THE PERFECT HIDING PLACE*

This legend tells us that in ancient times, every person on earth was a god. However, the main god, Brahma, got very upset by how the human beings were misusing their divinity. He felt they needed to be stripped of their godliness and that it should be hidden from them.

Brahma called for a meeting of a council of other leading gods in order to determine where to hide the divinity of the humans. Soon one god suggested that it be buried deep in the ground. However, the other gods argued that the people would learn how to dig into the earth and find it one day. Another god recommended placing it on the bottom of the sea. However, the council members countered that the humans would learn to dive deep into the ocean and eventually be able to retrieve it. A third god felt it should be placed on the highest mountain. But the council saw that the humans would also learn to climb, and they'd be able to get to it at some point. The gods were then puzzled because it seemed there was no spot on earth they could use as a reliable hiding place.

Brahma smiled, for he now had the answer. He proclaimed: "We shall hide it in their hearts, for it will be a long, long time before the humans would ever think of looking there. By the time they do, the people will finally have the wisdom to know how to use their divinity properly."

And so it was that each human being's divinity was hidden within their very own heart. But still over many centuries the people looked everywhere outside of themselves for the answers.

Remember This: As you explore your purpose, don't forget to look within for insights and solutions.

Wherever you go,
go with all your heart.
CONFUCIUS

□

Have you become more *conscious* about how you're spending the minutes of your day? Do you have the intention to live every day to its fullest? Part of being on purpose is recognizing that we are in charge of our own lives and that every moment offers us the gift of *choice*. However, *to live on purpose*, you must also have some idea of what you want. *You must have a purpose to live on purpose.* When we know what we are here to do, we can translate our larger purpose into deliberate daily acts that cultivate joy in our lives.

Each decision we make is either conscious and deliberate or an unconscious reaction. Asking yourself if your choice will keep **you on track** with your purpose will save you from making snap judgments and rash decisions. Ultimately, when you make the decisions that are right for you, they lead to a life of joyful purpose.

GROWTH EXERCISE

Are You Living On Purpose?

Is your purpose being served by the way you are currently choosing to live? Take the following quiz to find out.

1. **I am clear about my greatest talents and strengths.**

   Never   Rarely   About Half the Time   Often   Always

2. **I wake up in the morning excited about the day before me.**

   Never   Rarely   About Half the Time   Often   Always

3. **I know that who I am makes a difference in the world.**

   Never   Rarely   About Half the Time   Often   Always

4. **I enjoy what I do for its own sake, not just for what it gets me.**

   Never   Rarely   About Half the Time   Often   Always

5. **I know I am here to grow and evolve, and I see every day bringing me opportunities to heal and create.**

   Never   Rarely   About Half the Time   Often   Always

6. I hold myself accountable to living an authentic life that is directed by my core values.

Never   Rarely   About Half the Time   Often   Always

How did you do? For those who would like to do better, it can help to remember that living in the present moment keeps us from wasting our precious time worrying about the future, functioning on autopilot, or zoning out.

What role in your life gives you an inner sense of joy that carries you through the good times and the bad?

RETURNING TO THE SILENCE

As with our overall vision, a sense of our purpose is often strengthened when we spend time in silence. So it's important that we take time to be alone and still with ourselves so that truths about our purpose can be revealed. We can't be "on purpose" if we have not become aware. To increase your sense of purpose, some important questions to meditate on will be:

What am I here to learn?
What am I here to give?
What am I here to heal?

and

How do I want to be remembered?
What do I want people to say about me when I am gone?
How do I want to show up in the world?

and

Am I in alignment with what I love and value?
Am I in alignment with who I intend to be in the world?
Am I giving myself to situations that expand me?

These are not just one-time questions. They are meant to be asked on a weekly basis at least. We want to enjoy the process of unfolding our lives, not just focus on some ultimate static image of perfection. We want to enjoy *being* on purpose, rather than simply *arriving at* our purpose. Otherwise we will never be satisfied, because there's always going to be an area related to our purpose where we could improve. But if we enjoy the journey of evolving, we will have both the joy of growth and of discovery.

> Cherish the music that stirs in your heart,
> the beauty that forms in your mind...
> if you but remain true to them,
> your world will at last be built.
> JAMES ALLEN

☐

WHEN I GOT OFF TRACK

When Kirk and I opened the San Juan Capistrano gift store, Tara's Angels, we had the good intention of offering a place of love and inspiration to others who had lost a loved one. I was teaching once again and sharing my journey of recovery associated with the death of our dear daughter. It was very exciting to share our message of hope, and our store was very busy. We stayed with that retail business for seven years, and eventually there were problems.

During the troubled times, it dawned on me one day that I hate to shop. Some people love to go shopping, but I'd much rather have someone else do this for me. And there I was running a store! My heart just wasn't in the business anymore. Managing the store was just a job that didn't fulfill me.

I really had to listen to that call. I began to ask myself, *What am I here to learn and to give? What is my purpose?* At that point, I knew it wasn't to be the owner of a retail business.

With time and personal reflection, I realized that I needed to find a different way to give people the spiritual tools that would enable them to live a more positive life. Interestingly, I had already been taking ministerial classes, without the intention of starting a church. Somehow my inner guidance system had been directing me.

Operating on faith and with vision, I decided to lease a space where Kirk and I could open a church. We took a risk, and that's how our spiritual center was born: by answering and trusting my deep inner calling.

Are you living your purpose, or trying to fit into a life that someone else expects from you?

PURPOSE: OUR UNIQUE GIFT

Living out your purpose requires that you be centered in a strong sense of self. You are special in certain ways, as is everyone else. It's important to be truthful with yourself about where your particular strengths really lie. You don't want to try to be a great "someone else." We've all had the experience of encountering a person who is great at their job—perhaps an athlete, or a stand-up comic, or an artist—and thinking how we could never do the same thing as well. That person's purpose is not our own.

Living our purpose, using our special gifts, doesn't always take the form of our full-time profession or job. Sometimes we need to do other work to make a living, or something else may need our attention. But even in these cases, when we're on purpose, we can focus energy on something else to kindle the fire of purpose within us.

June, one of my congregants, has set her purpose on simply being a beneficial presence wherever she is. As a result, she is one of the most alive people I know. June is always there to help and to give. This woman is not missing out on anything because she is asleep. June's life has definitely become an adventure.

For others, their purpose *is* their profession or job. For instance, I recently attended a conference where I was reminded of the wonderful writings of Shel Silverstein, the popular children's book author. His best-selling titles include A *Light in the Attic, Where the Sidewalk Ends, The Giving Tree,* and *Falling Up.* When I was an elementary school teacher, I constantly used his work in my classes. One my favorites among his writings is the well-known poem titled "Woulda-Coulda-Shoulda," which talks about the things we think of doing and the regret we feel later when we've let opportunities pass us by.

Silverstein grabbed the opportunity to become a creative person by giving himself permission. At first it didn't fit the way he had been seeing himself. As a young teenager, he had wanted to become a baseball player, but that wasn't where his talents were. One day, Silverstein realized that he liked to write and draw. Since he had no mentors, he developed his own style. He went on to become very, very successful. Silverstein passed away in 1999, but his books continue to delight children and adults today.

One of the reasons for living is to leave a legacy. We each leave a *soul print* on the world when we leave. What kind of legacy are you leaving? Is it one of love, or something less positive? *What we choose to do with ourselves has an impact on others.*

We do not inherit the earth
from our ancestors,
we borrow it from our children.
NATIVE AMERICAN PROVERB

☐

GROWTH EXERCISE
What Would Living On Purpose Be Like?

To begin this visualization, picture yourself walking down a trail called *The Path of Purpose*. Up ahead, you see a bright light; it is the Light of Purpose. As you move further along the path into the Light of Purpose, imagine what it would be like to be *absolutely on purpose* in your life.

What would you be doing?

What would you be hearing?

What would you be seeing?

What would you be touching?

What would you be feeling?

Who is on the path with you when you are absolutely on purpose?

As you continue to visualize being on purpose, get really specific. What music do you hear? What foods are you eating? Are you living somewhere different? What activities are you involved in? How are you making a difference in the world?

Return to this visualization exercise time and time again to further expand a vision of your life that would include your purpose. Soon you will start to notice aspects of your visualization manifesting as the reality of your current life!

> Looking up gives light,
> although at first it makes you dizzy.
>
> RUMI

□

GROWTH EXERCISE

Seeing Our Purpose through Our Past Lives

Whether or not you believe in past lives, it can be fun to let your imagination run wild to picture who you might have been in centuries gone by. If you've ever seen the movie, *Defending Your Life*, you know that writer/director/actor Albert Brooks played on the idea of past lives by having an arcade in the story called the Past Lives Pavilion. There the characters played by Brooks and actress Meryl Streep were able to step into private booths to see moving pictures of themselves in previous incarnations.

For this exercise, you'll need to be content with just getting into a quiet place and opening yourself up to the possibilities. Let the feelings in your body allow you to "remember" who you were in previous lifetimes. See where you can go with this idea. When I've tried it, I've visualized myself as…

- An Egyptian princess
- A Benedictine monk
- A young girl selling flowers on the street, like in the movie "My Fair Lady"
- A worker in the fields on a farm

We are so multidimensional, yet so often think of ourselves as just being about one thing. But by using our imaginations in this way, we can tap into the parts of ourselves that we have taken for granted or otherwise overlooked. This process helps you move beyond the restrictions of your logical mind. Feel yourself expand as you imagine yourself in different roles. Tell yourself, I'll let myself be the nurse, or the pilot, or the cabaret dancer. What seems to fit? How can you use your imagination to expand your life? Try on something new.

This past lives exercise can help you tap into your purpose, or enhance how you're living out your purpose now, by showing you how to act upon it in a different way.

Living Wide Open: Landscapes of the Mind

A Poem by Dawna Markova

I will not die an unlived life.
I will not live in fear
of falling or catching fire.
I choose to inhabit my days,
to allow my living to open me,
to make me less afraid,
more accessible,
to loosen my heart
until it becomes a wing,
a torch, a promise.
I choose to risk my significance,
to live so that which came to me as seed
goes to the next as blossom,
and that which came to me as blossom,
goes on as fruit.

from Markova's book, *I Will Not Die an Unlived Life: Reclaiming Purpose and Passion*

When you take just one step toward Spirit, the Universe will rush in and take a thousand steps toward you to offer support.

WHAT'S NEXT?

All your work of preparation is about to pay off. It's time to act on your vision and your plans! The next chapter, "Taking Action by Sowing the Seeds of Your Future Garden," offers plenty of ideas about how to support yourself as you start to move forward with your action plan.

Learning to let yourself create is like learning to walk. The child artist must begin by crawling. Baby steps will follow and there will be falls...it is necessary to go gently and slowly...Mistakes are necessary! Stumbles are normal...Progress, not perfection, is what we should be asking of ourselves...

JULIA CAMERON

□

CHAPTER 7

Taking Action

Start Small and Build on Success

A journey of a thousand miles
must begin with a single step.

LAO TZU

Insanity is doing the same thing over and over
and expecting different results.

ALBERT EINSTEIN

Every journey starts with a solitary step. Sixth century B.C., Chinese philosopher Lao Tzu observed this simple truth that still inspires today. The first step is always the hardest. Why? It's the unknown.

Imagine a world that works in cooperation—no wars, crime, or poverty. This is a world where everyone loves what they do and has the health and vitality to do it; a world where the earth is respected and its resources honored. This may seem like a tall order, but I truly believe this type of world is attainable. We must collectively do our individual parts. Change will require moving beyond your current comfort zone. Though this may be difficult and challenging, it's a necessary part of creation. It's the essence of being green. This chapter provides tools to cope with this unavoidable aspect of change.

Renowned primatologist Jane Goodall recalled an acquaintance saying she wanted to do something to change the world, but the problems of the world were all too huge to tackle. Jane's response to the woman was, "Just find your piece of it."

Each of us has an integral part to play in the green movement, the movement of greater good. Who will you be? One of the tenets of permaculture is to start small and build on your successes. The critical part is simply to start. If the project seems too overwhelming, chances are you will procrastinate starting it or start then get frustrated and give up.

When designing for sustainable living, it's best to start small. Find what works in your own life and notice how that encourages your own patience, reflection, and feedback. Plant a small garden. Use the new earth-friendly products. Eat organic and local food. Pick one bird species living in your neighborhood and get to know it intimately instead of trying to learn about all of the wildlife in the surrounding area. If we try to do everything all at once, it usually becomes overwhelming and confusing. The same is true on the spiritual path. Pick one or two things to work on, get to know it, feel successful and then move on.

Cultivating a Sustainable Life: Start Small

In the movement towards sustainability, one of the most important actions we can take is to plant a garden of our own. A garden can provide us with food & beauty, and allow us to create our own healthy ecosystem in which to observe nature's connections.

I used to have a landscape design business called 'Green Insight Design'. Clients hired me and my partner to take out their lawn and plant organic, edible, native and medicinal gardens. It was so exciting and inspiring for us to take our shovels to the lawn and in place put in fruit trees, butterfly-attracting plants, vegetables, herbs, and flowers.

In order to have a successful garden, one must begin below the surface, in the soil. Rich soil is all about connections. Have you heard of mycorrhizae? A mycorrhizae is a symbiotic association between a fungus and the roots of a plant. They are an important component of soil life and soil chemistry. Mycorrhizae form a mutualistic relationship with the roots of most plants. When you plant a garden, make sure you are helping to create healthy soil by using organic soil inoculated with mycorizzhae.

Key Tips:
- Pick a place for your garden
- Make sure your garden gets an adequate amount of water, nutrients & sunlight
- Incorporate organic compost & mycorrizzhae into soil
- Get your hands on some organic seeds or plant starts
- Plant and watch your garden grow!

Resources
Geoff Lawton, Greening the Desert:
permaculture.org.au/2007/03/01/greening-the-desert-now-on-youtube

---

Taking action is a crucial step in growing your potential. Action manifests dreams. In the last two chapters, you prepared to take action by creating a mental image of how to grow your life — your *vision*. Without vision, you could end up moving around in circles, going nowhere. Instead, you are choosing to move in a particular direction.

In the previous chapter, we also covered *purpose*. Knowing your purpose helps direct you toward the right actions too. If your actions are not rooted in purpose, you get sidetracked. Actions must be rooted in *who you truly are*.

Compare this idea of being rooted in your purpose to how a tree is rooted in the soil. A deeply rooted tree, such as a white oak, can weather storms and hold its ground securely, constantly reaching upward. In contrast, a fast-growing tree, such as a desert willow, matures rapidly to provide quick relief from the sun, but then is blown over with the first windstorm.

The work you have done so far has been preparation for this chapter. You have turned on the light of awareness. The camera of your vision is rolling and now it's the time for *action*.

> It is never too late
> to be what you might have been.
> GEORGE ELIOT

☐

HOW DO YOU TALK TO YOURSELF?

As you begin to take action, think about what will support the steps you are taking. Are your thoughts self-propelling or self-repelling? Remember, thoughts are the nutrients that feed the quality of your life. How can you expect to cultivate joy, love, and miracles if your thoughts are not focused on appreciation, healing, peace, and growth?

The power of perception comes into play here. Self-talk trains us to view life as a possibility thinker or a problem thinker—to be living in *full choice* or *no choice*. It's all about how we regard our life and the world. For instance, you could view the field of your life as **fertile and cleared for new possibilities,** or as barren, stark, and empty.

The following exercise is designed to help you reframe thoughts about life on days when *the doing* gets difficult. Sometimes all that's needed to motivate you is a change of focus. Recognize that *whatever you focus on expands*! Change your thinking to change your life.

| GROWTH EXERCISE |

A Perspective Tune-Up

Step 1. Start by evaluating your current state of mind. How are you feeling *right now?* Tap into your present mood. Once you've tuned in, rate your state of being based on the following scale of one to seven (one being the highest level). Be authentic and objective. Don't worry about what anyone else might think. Remember, you're doing this in the company and privacy of your own heart and mind.

Ratings:
(1) Fantastic

(2) Great

(3) Good

(4) Okay

(5) Moody

(6) Down

(7) Depressed

Step 2. Work with the following statements. Copy some of the declarations down individually in your journal and then respond to them with your thoughts and answers.

1. There is beauty in this day. The beauty I see is_____.

2. Today I feel blessed because _____.

3. I know I can create my own experience. Today I choose to create more joy in my life by _____.

4. I know not everyone likes me, but there are people who look up to me with respect. The people who know and appreciate me include

_____.

5. I have confidence in the things I do well. Some of these things are

_____.

6. Thoughts of doubt, fear, and unworthiness are simply signs of being out of alignment with my wholeness. Some ways that I can more fully embrace my wholeness today include _____.

7. Today is the beginning of a new day. This is what I want to create:

_____.

8. I have solved some difficult problems in the past, and I will do so in the future. Some problems I successfully dealt with in the past include

_____.

9. I remember joyful times filled with laughter. The one that comes to mind now is _____.

10. A time of great ecstasy in my life was _____.

Step 3. Copy one or more of the following affirmations onto sticky notes. Place them in prominent spots within your living space.

I am in charge of my own life experience.

Sometimes I get caught up in the little things in my life and I forget about the possibilities that reside in every moment.

I am basically a joyous and loving person, capable of having a lot of fun.

I choose to create a joyful life by thinking thoughts of appreciation, healing, and love.

I am able to be self-confident, strong, and loving when I remember the truth about myself, that I am made of the creative essence of the Universe.

Step 4. Reevaluate how you feel. Rate your mood on the seven-point scale below. If you feel upset rather than lifted by this exercise, realize this is probably related to some valuable insights you've just gained.

Ratings:
   (1) Fantastic
   (2) Great
   (3) Good
   (4) Okay
   (5) Moody
   (6) Down
   (7) Depressed

When we are filled with inspiration and enthusiasm inspired by our vision, we are magnetized toward our dreams. It comes from the inside out.

We can experience each month as a single day lived over and over again or we can create thirty days that grow out of each other. It's all about how we look at our life.

_____ ◢ _____

SMALL STEPS CREATE THE MIRACLES

Life feels overwhelming at times. You wake up feeling passionate about cultivating joy in your life, then the magnitude of it all makes you want to dive back under the covers. If you want to grow, some of your energy must go into resisting urges to succumb to complacency—to the comfort of remaining in the rut of your current life. It takes courage to bend life into personal victory.

One secret to heading in a positive direction is taking small steps. Cut the things you want to do into small, easily manageable pieces, and then accomplish them one at a time. It's that simple to be on your way.

When I was a schoolteacher, my principal called me into his office one day. He told me he admired my ability to keep momentum going on a committee I had joined. The principal observed that I did this by asking the simple question, *What do we need to do next?* When he said this, I realized that by focusing the group's energy on identifying our next step, I was helping to achieve our goals. "What's next?" is a powerful question. Be sure you approach it with manageable, bite-sized answers.

Another important part of moving forward is celebrating every inch of progress you make. Become your best cheerleader. Instead of beating yourself up for what didn't get done, celebrate what was accomplished. Then you can enthusiastically look forward to the next small step, as well as the larger goal. Here's a special *cheer:*

> Yes, I got Spirit.
> I'm super and divine!
> Yes, I got Spirit and
> I'm doin' just fine.
> Hey, hey, hey,
> Get outta my way!
> I'm goin' for it—hey,
> and I got Spirit—Mine!
> HITTING THE WALL

□

Years ago, Clark Strand, a journalist, embarked on a spiritual journey entering a two-week silent retreat. Four days into silence, Strand felt he'd had enough. A monk happened by as Strand was packing to leave. Strand confided in the monk, telling him the idea of continuing for eight more days was more than he could handle. The monk smiled and said everyone felt that way. The trick was to just take it one day at a time.

Strand stayed. Eventually, he became a Zen Buddhist monk. Today he is the author of many wonderful books, including *Meditation Without Gurus: A Guide to the Heart of Practice*, *The Wooden Bowl: Simple Meditation in Everyday Life*, and *Seeds from a Birch Tree: Writing Haiku and the Spiritual Journey*. Strand has always maintained that a key to his breakthrough was tearing down his enlightening journey into smaller, doable pieces.

WHEN WE TAKE ON TOO MUCH

In their tune "The 59th Street Bridge Song (Feelin' Groovy)," Simon and Garfunkel sing about slowing down, being in the moment, and "feelin' groovy." We know how great it feels to embrace the moment and enjoy the beauty and power of *now*. However, as we enter the mode of creation, it's easy to be drawn out of the now into worry about the future. This anxiety can cause us to reach beyond the small step toward progress and take on more than we can handle. Kirk and I know this danger all too well. It's exactly what happened at our retail gift store, Tara's Angels.

The success of Tara's Angels took us by surprise. We quickly went from being a homespun family gift store to the subject of intense media coverage including television shows and cover stories in local and national magazines. People were intrigued by our message of love and healing, by the way we were learning about life and love through Tara's passing. Our intention in opening the store was to provide a place for healing for people dealing with the loss of loved ones. We wanted to be there for everyone who called or stopped by.

In addition to being a gift store, Tara's Angels offered workshops and lectures about healing and the power of love. The demand for Kirk's and my time and attention became overwhelming. Eventually we relinquished financial control of the business to an outside firm in order to relieve some of the pressure. This decision was a huge mistake—a choice that we are still recovering from today. It resulted in a breach of trust that precipitated our excruciating decision to close the original Tara's Angels store.

Whatever your vision is, remember that its manifestation will not be timed—it's not a race to the finish line. Cultivate your beautiful garden of joy in a way that is manageable for *you*, and enjoy the process of creation. Notice the wonder of your seeds of possibility breaking ground, your plants of potential budding, and their blossoms of action flowering before you. If you try to race the "manifestation clock," you may find yourself strangling your growth in your attempt to do too much all at once.

> We are not born all at once, but by bits.
> MARY ANTIN

☐

FUEL YOURSELF WITH FAITH

None of us has any guarantees about where a journey will lead us. When we have Faith, we know that any road we choose will take us to our good—and that this good is sometimes disguised as a difficult lesson we need to endure in order to manifest our vision. A key difference between winners and losers is the winner's faith in his or her ability to achieve goals. Have faith that the Universe will support you in taking the positive action necessary to manifest your dreams.

When Tara's Angels began to disintegrate, instead of wallowing in its failure, Kirk and I became more serious about being a source of inspiration and healing for people. We began studying to become ordained ministers with the larger goal of opening a spiritual center.

Despite the difficulties we experienced at the store, we were inspired by our faith in the idea of creating a spiritual gathering place. We knew in our hearts that this was the right thing to do. With the help of a realtor, we found a space in a commercial office building in Mission Viejo, California. We signed a one-year lease at $2,000 a month without ever having held a Sunday service. That was truly an act of Faith.

> Faith is taking the first step
> even when you can't see the whole staircase.
> MARTIN LUTHER KING, JR.

□

At first, our friends and supporters found it hard to believe that the indifferent office space we had rented could be turned into a warm and welcoming spiritual center. With faith, I told them, "You just wait and see." With their help, we began to tear down walls to create a large interior area where people could gather. Soon there were only a few finishing touches to complete before we were ready to open the doors.

Our first church service was on Mother's Day, May 9, 1999. Through word of mouth and personal invitations to friends and family, our initial service drew over ninety guests.

Our spiritual center provided an opportunity for Kirk to act with faith in pursuing his own personal dream. Kirk never believed he could have the musical career he had always dreamed of and successfully provide for a family. Although he had a contemporary music band (Moore & Moore) when we met and fell in love in our twenties, Kirk eventually let it go in order to pursue a more stable profession and support his young family. Our new church opened up the possibility for him to become musical director. With faith, Kirk was able to set free the music in his soul. Today, as assistant minister and musical director, Kirk leads our church choir, directing them with passion and commitment.

What is it that you could achieve if you had a little more *faith?*

Remember This: A scared little seed needs to grow in the darkness before it can break through the soil's surface and rise beautifully out of the earth. What is it that you could achieve if you had a little more faith?

Are You Committed to Your Dream?
The Crucial Role of Commitment

Don't wait for someone else
to make your life terrific.
That's your job.
ANONYMOUS

□

What does it take to live a life of growth and transformation? Commitment! It's a term that evokes strong reactions. Some people look at it as meaning oppressive obligation with no turning back. Others simply shy away from any conversation about it.

Commitment is empowering. It determines the quality of our lives. Commitments make a statement about our intentions.

When I married Kirk, I didn't marry "for life," I married "for good." I made a commitment that I was willing to do what was necessary and appropriate through the years in order to learn, heal, and mend my marriage when and if necessary. I told myself that if there was ever a time I didn't feel the good outweighed the bad—even though I'd done all that I could to heal and mend our relationship—I would release it.

My personal commitment, made at the beginning of my marriage to Kirk, is what has given me the abiding energy and strength to foster a relationship for more than thirty years. Our marriage has survived many deaths, a bankruptcy, job losses, and a variety of other serious issues. Thankfully, today it is still thriving and growing.

What we commit to needs to be in line with our purpose, dreams, and desires. I make commitments easily because of their inherent power. Because our commitments are an expression of who we are, they hold the power to mold and shape our own lives—and the world.

There is no such thing as 99 percent commitment. The 1 percent hesitancy gives us an out, and the ego always wants an out. Make a commitment to yourself today with your entire being, heart, and spirit.

Being Open to Synchronicities

Being steadfastly committed to our dreams doesn't mean being totally inflexible. Commitment doesn't come with blinders. No matter how clear your vision and expectations are, your dreams won't unfold in the precise way you think it's going to happen. Being green and living your best life requires that you not only have a vision, but keep your ears and eyes alert for synchronistic messages from the Universe about your vision. If you receive information that a different action makes more sense, then go with it. Be open to *all* possibilities.

We need to have a mind that is
open to everything and attached to nothing.

DR. WAYNE W. DYER

□

GROWTH EXERCISE:
Free Yourself of Fear

Often the only thing that keeps you from taking the next step is fear. Fear of the unknown and what it might demand of you. Fear of failure. Fear of what you might have to give up in order to achieve your dreams. Fear of your innate greatness. Fear of envy. Fear upon fear upon fear.

If we remain stuck in our fears, we become paralyzed—the opposite of action, which is our goal. The next time you feel afraid, try one or more of these *antidotes for fear*.

Antidote #1: Humor. Angels can fly because they take themselves lightly. When you're afraid, try injecting humor into the situation. Don't take yourself so seriously. Laugh it off. So what if you don't do something perfectly. Your foible may provide hours of laughter—and laughter is great medicine.

Antidote #2: Act "as if." When fear crops up, try acting confident. Fill yourself up with positive thoughts and feelings. See yourself successfully doing what needs to be done. How would success make you feel? How would you act? Expect success. Go for the feeling that you would have if the goal were already achieved.

Antidote #3: Face fear. Write down your worst fears. This may not be easy, but once the list is complete, decide which fears aren't real and cross them off the list. Develop a plan to deal with the remaining fears that are real to you. These may include things you can change, as well as things beyond your control that you might cope with in a better way with some unbiased thought.

Antidote #4: Know that fear is fodder for growth. A change in mindset can be helpful to overcome fear. Do your best to eliminate the word "failure" from your vocabulary. Instead of looking at mistakes as failures, discover what you need to learn from them. See what you could do differently. It's normal to make mistakes when you try something new. Really, *it's* OK. The trick to turning mistakes into something positive is to identify and imprint the lessons learned from them.

Antidote #5: Do something new every day. Take small daily risks. Try a different route to work, sample a new type of ethnic food, watch a TV show you've never seen before, experiment with a new type of exercise. Get used to taking small risks and see what happens. Increasing your risk tolerance helps to expand horizons and enables you to think more creatively.

Antidote #6: Adjust your perspective. If you're worried about something, ask yourself, *What difference will this make six years from now?* If it would make a significant difference, then begin working on resolution. If not, recognize where it fits into your priorities. If it's not important, let it go.

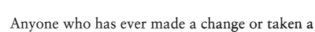

Anyone who has ever made a change or taken a
chance has felt fear. It's an innate part of being human.
Think of someone who has achieved a goal.
That person understood
that fear itself is irrelevant.

SUSAN JEFFERS

☐

GROWTH EXERCISE

Journaling Your Progress Daily

In the process of manifesting your vision, it's helpful to take stock of progress periodically. Do this once a day in the evening. At the end of the day, grab your journal or sit down at the computer, and do this exercise. If it's too hard to make time for the practice every day, then do it as often as you can.

First, record your blessings. Note at least five of them. Next, write some words of celebration for the small steps you accomplished during this period. Then write responses to some of the following questions. Choose the ones that resonate in this moment.

Where did I resist taking appropriate and healthy action to further my vision?

Where did my fear take over my life?

Where did fear override my Faith?

How did I act inauthentically?

Was I paralyzed by wondering what other people would think of me? Did I wonder if I had what it takes to achieve my dream?

What action am I able to take next to assist in manifesting my vision?

To end the practice, take five minutes to visualize successfully taking the next step. Fill yourself up with the feelings you would have if this step were already accomplished. Finally, relax for a moment with slow, easy breaths before returning to your evening activities.

WHAT'S NEXT?

As you start to take action to cultivate joy, you must communicate with others about your envisioned changes. This helps people adjust to the new as it begins to take shape and gives them information about how they can be supportive. It takes courage to be different and to create a new life, because not everyone will be happy that you are evolving in fresh ways. Chapter 8 will help you find the courage to be real with others as you grow into joyful purpose.

Green Intention Affirmation:
*I know everything I need to know right now,
and I am always ready to learn more.*

All the power of the Universe is with you.
Feel it, know it, and then
act as though it were true.
ERNEST HOLMES

□

Communicating Plans

All Things are Connected

Union gives strength.
AESOP

Get around the right people.
Associate with positive, goal-oriented people
who encourage and inspire you.
BRIAN TRACY

Until now, your vision has largely been expanding internally. Now it's time to allow that creative energy to expand. As you begin to take action to manifest your dreams, you will communicate your intentions more widely and naturally involve others. You will transition from vibrating the energy of your plans in a small way to a much larger way.

Vibrational Energy

Everything is made of energy. We are energetic beings. Energy vibrates, creating a magnetic field. As we vibrate, or send out signals, we attract to us what we are putting out. This is one of the great laws of the Universe: The Law of Attraction. Like the great mystics have said, "It is done unto us as we believe; what we reap so shall we sow; ask and it is given." Simply put, we are kind of like big magnets.

As self-aware beings, we are able to adjust our vibrational level by becoming aware of our thoughts and feelings and making adjustments in them so that we are vibrating "good vibes" in alignment with what we want to create in our lives. In manifesting our dreams, we want to extend our vibration out to magnify it toward our intentions, dreams, and goals. Although making our intentions clear and involving others will bring blessings, it can also be tricky and challenging.

> Forget safety.
> Live where you fear to live.
> Destroy your reputation.
> Be notorious.
>
> RUMI

☐

OWNING OUR REINVENTED SELVES

Communicating our plans requires us to have the courage to speak about what we are doing and own it. By committing to a green life, you are reinventing yourself—creating a fresh, new you. Through communicating about this self in the world, you can draw in added support and energy. There is abundant power to connect with others via words and action.

Before you communicate your reinvention, you must be centered in your belief that it is so. Use Rumi's poem to inspire yourself about living your life always as an expanding, evolving human being.

First, this insightful Persian poet says that reinvention will require that you "forget safety." I believe this means stepping out of the box of homogenized thinking. As you change, you must be self-directed, moving *beyond* conducting yourself according to other people's expectations. Forget creating your self safely, based simply on what others would like or accept you to be.

Next, Rumi says that you must live where you fear to tread. I interpret this as pushing out the edges of our lives. You must free yourself of your old limitations. Find a fresh way to face your fears and step into the growth mandated by your dreams.

Calling on you to "destroy your reputation," Rumi points out that in reinvention, you must give yourself permission to break out of the self that is a reflection of what others want from you. Abandon who you think you are, who others think you are, and become who you truly are supposed to be in the Divine plan. Be the person your Spirit directs you to be.

Finally, Rumi advises that you "be notorious." I had to think about that one. When I looked up "notorious" in the dictionary, I discovered that it means to be known widely, *especially unfavorably*. I wasn't sure I wanted to do that. But then I realized that I *am willing* to be seen in an unfavorable way in the eyes of "race consciousness" — the mentality that says, "This is the way it has always been done. You must do it the traditional way." To that end, I am willing to reply, "It doesn't work for me." I want to be unfavorable to that way of thinking.

My beautiful daughter, Deanna, is the queen of outrageous, out-of-the-box thinking. When she lost her sister she was twelve years old. She and Tara were best friends and opposites. They fit beautifully together to create wholeness. I know Deanna felt like she lost part of herself when Tara left so suddenly. She needed to go on a deep search to find her true self. She said to me not long after Tara's death that her great fear was that I would hold onto her so tight because of my fear that I might lose her, too.

Deanna and I made an agreement then and there that if she gave me very little to worry about I would not clip her wings, but let her fly. I often wondered why I made that agreement, because she asked for some outrageous things. She found very little meaning in high school, except for her joy in playing soccer. She had always loved learning, but life just didn't make sense anymore. She looked to college as a time of real learning. However, when she started college, what she found was high school partying—expanded. She called often from her dorm crying, "Mom there's got to be more than this."

Deanna made a decision at that time that her learning was going to be experiential. I was surprised to find she had made a plan to travel to Africa by herself, at eighteen, to study at the Cheetah Conservation Fund in Namibia. We had made an agreement. I had to let her go. As her dad and I put her on the airplane, we all three cried. We knew we wouldn't speak to her for some time. And we knew her sister was watching over her.

About three weeks later, I received a letter from her saying she felt like she was in the cradle of creation and it was an unbelievable experience. She said she would call us in a couple of weeks when she got to a city. When she called I told her to send us the information of when and where to meet her in Africa and we would be there. I couldn't imagine not being able to share that experience with my courageous and brilliant daughter. She sent the information. We went, and it was the most expansive time of my life. Deanna was our guide, and to this day the beauty of the country and the magnificence of the animals hold a special place in my heart.

Reinvention can be confusing because you find yourself doing things in different ways. There's something disconcerting about this. The old habitual self will become alarmed and protest, *Hey, wait a minute. What's going on? I want to be comfortable. You're messing things up!* But then the moment comes when you realize that you are freeing yourself. And while this is exciting, it isn't always comfortable. When you understand and embrace the reasons that you reinvented yourself in the first place, you can find the courage to articulate your reinvention to the world.

GROWTH EXERCISE
Believing in Your Vision Meditation

Because you are the ambassador—the PR agent—for your vision, it's important to be rooted in belief in the dreams you're growing. Here is a meditation to further strengthen your resolve and self-confidence.

To start, find a place that represents peace and safety for you. It could be a cozy couch or a favorite room. It might be the chair at your desk during a break. Wherever it is, just sit there and get comfortable for a minute or two—perhaps taking off your shoes as you quiet your mind. It might be nice to light a candle and put on some soft music, if possible.

Begin your meditation with focused breathing. Breathe in fully, pulling the air down deeply into your stomach, and then hold your breath for a few seconds. Exhale, releasing any tension, confusion, or worry. Allow yourself to be present in the moment.

Let your mind rest in loving heart energy. Be aware of the presence of Spirit and the Universal force that surrounds and infuses you with creative energy. After you are relaxed and aware of the presence of an infinite creativity that surrounds and fills you, start slowly speaking internally about your vision. Say the following in the present tense as if the following things are already a part of your life:

I am (describe your vision—for example, "open to changing my career)."

I am focused on achieving my Good.

I am filled with creative ideas.

Everything I need comes to me easily and effortlessly.

I am aware of all I need to know and everything unfolds in perfect timing.

Now visualize yourself manifesting your vision in your mind's eye. See yourself and all those involved being joyful as together you bring your vision to life. See the creative energy of your vision working through you to bring it to physical manifestation. See the joy and blessing that your vision brings both to you and to all those it touches.

Remember This: It is a process to train your subconscious mind to believe in your dreams and intentions so that your will is unshakable. When your vision is firmly planted in your mind and body, you will not go off course—no matter what circumstances present themselves in your life.

NAYSAYERS AND SUPPORTERS

As you share your vision, you will encounter people who support your new Spirit-directed life and people who condemn it. I've had these experiences of confronting naysayers in my own life.

Can you imagine the resistance I received when I began to tell people that I was leaving the teaching profession after twenty years to open an "angel store"? Some people said, "You're what? Leaving the security of teaching? Have you lost every speck of common sense that was ever in your head?"

I was so aligned with purpose that I knew I needed to take this next step or die. I simply couldn't live any other way. So I was strong enough to withstand all the negative thoughts and comments people were slinging at me. I had prayed. I had visioned. I had meditated and become clear. Opening the store was the next step that I *had* to take. After gaining a spiritual perspective on Tara's death, I knew that I wanted to share my message of hope with others who had lost a loved one.

Again, we come to the importance of listening to our inner guidance system, like a flower turning its face to the sun. Using it, you become clear in your purpose, gain an idea for manifesting it, and begin to believe in it with every fiber of your being. Once you've embodied your dream in this way, you are ready to communicate it.

With the help of *The Green Intention*, you have committed to growing your possibilities. You've let go of your unworthiness. You've prepared for new growth. You've strengthened yourself with the power of your Vision and Purpose. You're starting to take action. Now take the next step—*become your Vision by speaking it.*

> Life is a banquet
> but most poor suckers
> are starving to death!
> AUNTIE MAME

☐

THE IMPORTANCE OF ASKING

This chapter on communicating your plans follows the chapter on taking action. Why? Picture this scenario. You want to go out to eat. You take the action of going to one of your favorite restaurants. Do you expect to be served without looking at a menu and asking for what you want? *Of course not.* That's what life is like. In order to receive, you must ask for what you want.

In fact, one of the key points in any relationship—whether it is with a friend, a spouse, a coworker, or anyone—is asking for what you want. Other people cannot read your mind and figure out what you need. Consider all the work you have had to do to figure out what is right for you. And that's you, the person who knows you better than anyone else. You must help others to see your vision through your eyes by talking about it.

What happens when we force others to try to figure out what we want from them without communicating our needs? They're not going to get it quite right. Have you had that experience before in your relationships? You have someone in your world who is meeting many of your needs, but sometimes you think their answers and actions are a little off the mark. They don't quite fit *you*. Their solutions may be right for how they see you, or what they believe would be good for you. But if you don't ask, you risk ending up with a less than optimal result.

It is amazing when I am counseling people, how few really know how to ask for what they want. There is a built-in expectation that because someone loves us they should know what we want. People often do not realize that we can only see situations from our own framework and through the lenses of our own experiences. It sheds a whole new light on things when people we love and care about actually tell us what they want. When they do, what a difference it makes in the relationship.

Give some thought to what you might tell others to make them truly be supportive of you. How can you get them on track? Come up with some effective and appropriate requests. Do you need to communicate to a friend that you'll be taking more time and space for yourself in order to grow your dreams? Do you want time with your partner to talk out some ideas you have? Could you exchange services with another professional, or do you need to discuss the possibility of someone working for you?

Remember, if you don't ask, you get no answer. If you want your needs to be met, first make them known.

Ask, and it shall be given you;
Seek, and ye shall find;
Knock and it shall be opened unto you.
For every one that asketh, receiveth, and he who seeketh, find-
eth, and to him who knocketh, the door shall be opened.

MATTHEW 7:7

□

CALLING FORTH SUPPORT FOR THE CONGREGANT

Before departing on a Caribbean vacation, I realized that I needed to arrange for emotional support for one of our congregants who had been very ill. While stopping by to see her I realized that much of her pain during my absence might be related to loneliness. I had been visiting her often, but now I would be gone for ten days. I didn't want loneliness to cause her condition to spiral downward.

I told her my intention was to have one person come by for an hour or two every day. That way, she would look forward to their company. And after they left, she could think about the conversation and activities they shared.

When I got back to my office that day, I put my intention out there. I told my office manager and a female visitor about the beloved congregant and her illness. Both women said they would go see her. They also spread the word, and soon we had two weeks' worth of volunteers! People quickly stepped up to be supportive. It was incredibly fulfilling for me. If I had said nothing, our congregant could have gone unsupported, and her ill state of health could have worsened.

When I shared this need with the two women in my office, I embodied the necessity of the request. I strongly felt my wish for the congregant to feel loved and taken care of. The thought wasn't just in my mind, but also in my heart. I felt the need strongly inside of myself, and the two women picked up on my energy. My strong belief that this was a worthy thing to do enabled them to accept it for themselves.

With little effort, our congregant was supported. The means was basically a communication of intention and plans. It felt wonderful to make the companionship possible—a positive outcome for all of us.

> Your task is not to seek for love,
> but merely to seek and find
> all the barriers within yourself
> that you have built against it.
>
> RUMI

□

BEING OPEN TO RECEIVE

We miss many miracles in our lives because we're not open to receiving them. Perhaps we're stuck in the past, or worried about the future, so we don't see the wonderfulness that is there in the moment. Nothing works if you're not open to it. Realize that while the Universe may be knocking at the door to deliver your dreams, you may be blocking its energy and gifts by closing it.

Be willing to accept your gifts. If you don't accept them, it's the same as if you never asked for them in the first place. I've observed that people can be terribly afraid of accepting their good. They worry, *Oh gosh, if all this good comes into my life, maybe people won't like me. They'll be jealous.* Or, *If I accept all of my good, then I will stand out. I won't be part of the crowd.* They're afraid of being attacked. People become so afraid of having what they want that they completely shut down.

Keep this in mind: *I, like everyone else, deserve a good life. More than that, I deserve a wonderful, abundant life.*

Accepting your good is not selfish, though it might feel that way at first because of your conditioning. Instead, the actual truth is that you have more to give when you give to yourself first.

When you can accept all the good that is there for you—and you are willing to create a positive, abundant life—then, by example and through your new resourcefulness, you develop that possibility for others. I really do believe that we are here to support one another. In the long run, it's not just about having the good for ourselves. True prosperity is having the ability to help one another and be connected.

DON'T BE DEFEATED BY OTHERS' THOUGHTS

When you hear basketball superstar Michael Jordan's name mentioned in a news report or conversation, you might think of grace, innovation, and style on the court, a championship-level sports professional, a player loved by his many fans, and/or a man who is now supporting the development of other young players. Back when he was a sophomore at Laney High School in Wilmington, North Carolina, this two-time Olympic medalist had to face being cut from his varsity team.

For Jordan, this became a defining moment. He didn't let others set the bar for how well he would play basketball. He wasn't going to diminish himself based on how someone else saw him. Instead he decided that he would use this rejection as fuel to push himself to work harder.

Michael Jordan was not going to be defeated. He tried harder, because he knew his purpose was to play basketball. He practiced for hours and hours. "Whenever I was working out and got tired and figured I ought to stop, I'd close my eyes and see that list in the locker room without my name on it. And that usually got me going again."

And look at what he was able to accomplish. Within just a year of that early rejection, Jordan was back on the varsity team in high school, and he soon went on to attend the University of North Carolina. In 1984, he headed up the U.S. Men's Olympic Basketball Team and took home a gold medal. When he left college that year, Jordan joined the National Basketball Association, where he became known as one of the greatest players of all time. His amazing performances on the NBA circuit prompted even fellow superstar Magic Johnson to remark, "There's Michael Jordan, and then there is the rest of us." In 1992, Jordan returned to the Olympics to take another medal in basketball.

When someone criticizes your courage to step into your dream, this reflects their fears. They are unable to see the possibilities you're aware of in the same way you do. Like Michael Jordan, you can keep your mind on your vision, and not allow any critic to steer you off course. Stay empowered and feel the strength that comes from being rooted in your purpose.

> Stay focused and dedicated.
> The game has its ups and downs,
> but you can never lose focus
> of your individual goals.
> MICHAEL JORDAN

□

GIVING AND COMPLETING THE CIRCLE

This chapter began by discussing radiating the energy of your vision out into the world. One way to jumpstart the energy flow and get it going in a circular pattern—from you out to others and then back to yourself—is to be a *giver*. Throughout the ages, every wise culture has known that in order to receive, a person must give. This truth is reflected in such common sayings that we know today as,

What goes around comes around.

You have to reap before you can sow.

Do you expect always to be exalted by being on the receiving end? Or are you also willing to be humble, to give as well as to receive? It's hard for people to give to someone who continually acts superior or expectant in an arrogant way. Instead of copping a "me first" attitude, recall Bob Dylan's famous song, "Gotta Serve Somebody."

An interesting phenomenon occurs when we create this sort of circular energy pattern by giving. The resources that are available can actually expand as the energy flows around the circle. A synergy is created, and the resulting total amount of energy becomes greater than that which was originally contributed.

You can cultivate the habit of giving by adopting the following practices:

1. Look for ways to give on a regular, ongoing basis. Does a neighbor need a smile in passing? Could you help a friend face a challenge? Could you reach out and forgive a family member today? Remember, you can give of your time, heart, mind, and physical/nonphysical resources.

2. When someone gives to you, find a way to give back to them or someone else. What are their goals, and how can you help them move a step closer? Does your supporter need a fun friend for a refreshing night out? An open compassionate listener? A last-minute helper on their own project? If you can't help them, who else in your world needs support?

3. Don't panic when your resources seem to be low. Instead, ask, "What is the next step I need to take?" and "How can I give today?"

As you become more engaged in the circle of giving, it will be interesting for you to observe how energy is exchanged in the Universe. You shouldn't expect the person who gives back to you to be the same person that you gave to in the first place. This is often part of the fun—enjoying the surprise of receiving from an unexpected source. It's a big Universe and your Good can come from many unexpected places.

Of course, giving is simply good for the soul. That's the meaning behind the popular saying, "Giving is its own reward." Yes, it can be deeply soul warming to give and see another spirit benefit. For additional ideas on giving, see the book *The Giving Heart: Unlocking the Transformative Power of Generosity in Your Life* by M. J. Ryan.

Remember This: True prosperity is not about how much money you make. It's the ability to help one another and be connected.

Green Intention Affirmations: Receiving Support

I am open to the abundant gifts of the Universe.

I know what I can do and where I need support.

I ask for the support I need.

I allow Abundance and Good to flow through me.

I receive all the support I want and need.

I act with high intention and purposeful awareness.

I accept my good right now.

I make every act an act of love and respect for all life.

I am powerful. I am worthy. I am loveable. I am free.

According to Albert Einstein, the one question that will most determine the quality of our life is, "Is the Universe a friendly place?" Choose to say, "Yes," and see it!

WHAT'S NEXT?

As our dreams begin to grow, they will require care. But when we can be excited about what we are creating, this care is done with joy. Chapter 9 helps you condition your mind to live joyfully. It also assists you in remaining flexible in order to evolve and to let your good take unexpected turns when necessary. You'll also learn how to set priorities and face challenges.

> There's no limit possible
> to the expansion of each one of us.
> CHARLES M. SCHWAB

☐

CHAPTER 9

Emergence

The Only Constant is Change

This is the great Mystery, the limitless wonder of the Universe—
that which out of nothing can make something.

ERNEST HOLMES

Men are born soft and supple;
dead, they are stiff and hard.
Plants are born tender and pliant;
dead, they are brittle and dry.
Thus whoever is stiff and inflexible
is a disciple of death.
Whoever is soft and yielding is a disciple of life.
The hard and stiff will be broken.
The soft and supple will prevail.

LAO-TZU

You've designed your plan—your vision—and now it's starting to roll out. Sprouts have popped up out of the soil, and they are growing. You are taking pride in all you've accomplished with the support of the Universe.

At the same time, you understand this manifestation of your dream will need tending as it continues to emerge and evolve. To assist you in these efforts, Chapter 9 offers ideas for cultivating your garden of joy after it has taken root and is growing over time.

Unhappiness ultimately arises not from the circumstances of
your life, but from the conditioning of your mind.

ECKHART TOLLE

□

GROWTH EXERCISE

Conditioning Our Minds for Joy

As your vision begins to manifest, condition your mind everyday to be joyful about growing into something new and being in the process of creation. To start, consider Ernest Holmes' definition of joy as an emotion excited by the expectancy of good. I love this definition because what I want for you is even beyond the idea of happiness. The feeling of happiness is only transitory, and it's an emotion that results from something good happening in the moment. But joy is something that we can hold within ourselves all of the time. We can know that no matter what is happening, there is something good for us in it—a gift waiting to be revealed.

To begin this daily practice, sit comfortably in a quiet place where you won't be interrupted. Meditate on the knowledge that there is an Infinite Intelligence surrounding you. Draw this Infinite Intelligence in through your crown chakra, filling yourself up to the point of overflowing, only to be aware once again that you are surrounded by light. Call in the wisdom of this light[1] as it flows around, in, through, and out of you, around, in, through, and out of you—again and again. Feel the intensity of its healing nature as you bathe yourself and luxuriate in the light.

Bring the light in, and say, *Mind, be healed, be renewed, and be open to all the good that is ever present.* Then let go of all the limitations, the past experiences, all the stuff that keeps you blocked—just release it into that Infinite Intelligence

---

1 You may want to think of the light as a white refreshing glow. Or you might find that a certain healing color resonates with you—perhaps yellow, or orange, or turquoise. Decide whether a white light feels best for you for this practice, or if another color brings more healing energy to you. And then go with whichever you prefer.

that only knows to heal. As you are releasing, notice the dependability of your breathing as air goes in and out, in and out, and in and out. Relax, take in one more big deep breath, and then let go of more limiting material as you allow yourself to utter an expressive sigh... *Aaaaaaahhhhhh.* Continue to release as you breathe in and out until you feel you've done enough cleansing work for this session.

And if you have a painful heart— because you've been judged or something has happened to cause sadness—bring the light of Infinite Intelligence into your heart. Say, *Heart, be healed. Be renewed. Be open to the love that is ever present.* And keep breathing. As you breathe, recognize the pain and then let it go.

Or perhaps there is a part of your body that needs special attention. Maybe there are aches, pains, or illnesses in your body. Find the place that's having trouble, and just bring the light in and let it hover there awhile. Say, *Body, be healed. Be renewed. Be open to rejuvenation and a return to vibrant health.* Breathe. Relax and feel the healing energy doing its loving work.

Now say, *My Mind is Good. My Body is open to the healing that is ever available. I let it be, and so it is. Thank you Infinite Intelligence for your healing way that is always available to meet my needs.*

―――――――――――――――――― ✧ ――――――――――――――――――

There is a divine and universal information bank that is readily available to you anytime and anywhere. It has been designed to meet your needs. It can be printed on your mind or on your heart. It can be retrieved by anyone who holds the basic knowledge that God is the software! You are the hard drive!

IYANLA VANZANT

☐

ALLOWING EXPANSION AND GROWTH

When a seed is planted, it cannot completely grasp the glory of its coming evolution. Yet its inherent nature is to grow and to become its full potential. The same is true for humans. The difference is that we have been given free will and thus have a choice in every moment whether we will allow our potential to expand and take hold, or if we will hang on to a less-desirable situation.

Conscious Expansion and Growth

The Amazon rainforest sustains one of the richest concentrations of plant and animal biological diversity in the world. The Amazon rainforest has been called the lungs of our planet, because it continuously recycles carbon dioxide and exhales oxygen. The tropical rainforests are the single greatest terrestrial source of air that we breathe.

Native peoples of the Amazon rainforest have used different plants for centuries as medicines for their health and survival. Almost half of the medicinal compounds we use every day are derived from plants endemic to the tropical rainforest. A major concern for the Amazon region is the future of its indigenous people and their vast knowledge of their biological biodiversity. In the past 500 years the indigenous population has decreased dramatically, with only about 200,000 indigenous people living in their bioregions. With the loss of these people goes a several generations of knowledge of medicinal species of plants and organisms.

Last year I took my first journey to South America to explore and learn about the chocolate agriculture and industry. I stayed in Ecuador, and travelled extensively through the country on my short visit. On the last two days of my trip, I took a spontaneous adventure into the Amazon rainforest, something that I wanted to do, but didn't make plans ahead of time or know how it was going to happen. We were led by a Shuar shaman into his home territory to spend time with his family and learn about their "botanical garden." This was the best example of a garden I have seen! The abundance of the Amazon provided us with all of the food and medicine we needed during our stay.

These people are truly tending the wild forests to keep the balance and provide for their families. I felt so connected and inspired by the abundance and vibrancy of the jungle, yet disheartened by the encroaching roads, cattle ranches, oil companies, and industrial farms that are eating away little by little into the forest. It made me wonder if the products and benefits derived from these resources are worth the efforts to attain them.

By understanding our needs for the products we consume and the source of the materials and resources they require, we become conscious of our role in the health of our global ecological balance.

What to do?

- Support companies, organizations and people that protect and regenerate the rainforests.
- Make sure that tropical goods like coffee, tea, chocolate, bananas, & vanilla come from organic & fair trade verified sources.
- Become a vegetarian (or practice at least a few days per week)
- Check that wood material for flooring & building are Forest Stewardship Council (FSC) certified.
- Be fully informed about where materials, supplies & products that you purchase come from.
- Protect people & places that live in the forests & hold valuable knowledge.
- Donate to causes & take part in efforts that plant trees & reforest the earth.

Resources:
Amazon Watch: www.amazonwatch.org
Amazon Conservation Team: www.amazonteam.org
Pachamama Alliance: www.pachamama.org
Forest Stewardship Council:

It takes courage to grow consciously, especially if your physical eyes can see no other way for growth to happen. At the very least you can imagine the result and see its image in your mind. You can hold a space for the vision that you want to manifest.

The story of the establishment and expansion of our Spiritual Center starts with my husband Kirk and me attending a church for ten years. We were very active there, and the minister became a dear friend. It was at this church that I received my spiritual training and underwent my ministerial studies.

Soon after I received my ministerial license, I found out that my beloved minister had decided to retire. I questioned who would take her place and entertained the idea that it might be me. I turned in my paperwork to become a candidate for the senior minister position at the church. When the Nominating Committee did not accept my application, I felt deeply hurt by those I considered family. On top of that, I was not told directly—only learned the news at a member meeting where there was discussion about the qualifications for the new minister—which did not describe me.

In painful times, it takes tremendous trust and courage to step on the path of uncertainty, to surrender, and to allow Spirit to guide you. When I was rejected by our church, the thought of creating and expanding a church of our own seemed like a monumental task. I had to break my dream into manageable steps (see Chapter 7, "Taking Action by Sowing the Seeds of Your Future Garden"). I asked myself: *What is the next best step for me?*

The voice I heard said, "Rent a space where you could establish a church." And so I contacted a friend who was a real estate agent and off we went in search of a good location. We found a perfect place for our church right away. Kirk and I signed the papers, taking on a $2,000-a-month lease, without even having a congregation. I was allowing the voice of Spirit to guide me every step of the way.

You'll see it when you believe it.
DR. WAYNE W. DYER

☐

We opened The Center for Universal Truth on Mother's Day 1999. Ninety people attended that first service, and we grew from there. I simply trusted that something greater wanted to be created. Kirk and I didn't know how we were going to grow a church. It wasn't anything we had ever done in our lives, but we felt guided and continued to take the next appropriate and manageable step along the way. We are still taking those steps today.

It's been a continual process of growing and learning, and asking the right questions. We are aware that we don't know everything, and allow the answers to come to us. We've known better than to think that we could control everything. And in that way, we haven't blocked the incoming flow of something much greater than what we are at any given time.

We stayed at that first location for a few years. Then, once again we had to take a leap of faith when it was time to move into a larger space. We had to step out with trust and keep asking, *What is the next right step?*

We are looking for an even larger new space. The answer we're getting is our next step is to move into a facility that can accommodate an even larger congregation. I simply allow myself to be in the wonder of it. I think to myself: *Well, I wonder what it's going to look like. I wonder what it's going to feel like operating out of there.* I imagine it, I vision it, and I feel all the wonderful feelings that surround it. I prepare myself to surrender absolutely to the surprise of it all. My excitement keeps the positive energy going.

The Universe has guided me and directed me about our Center, and I have trusted the flow. At the same time, we have been making grounded decisions. We've made choices that are based in logic and reason. We haven't gone flying off into the ether, but instead have been stretching and growing.

Someday, Kirk and I would like to have a church campus. We see the campus having a spiritual center, a school, and an organic restaurant. Is this our next right step? No. Is it totally out of the question? No. We plan to build toward it over the years. In the meantime, we take reasonable interim steps on the path to creating our campus.

To keep yourself in the faith, in a state of belief in the growth of your vision, it's helpful to have an affirmation that you can pull out of your pocket at any time. Lately for me, it's been: *Thy grace is my sufficiency.* This short affirmation tells me that the Universe has guided and directed me, and that I have to trust in the flow. Spirit will not abandon me. Some other helpful affirmations for expanding your vision are:

There is a Divine plan at work in my life.

I trust in the processes of life and I am safe.

With humble gratitude, I graciously accept my Good.

Remember This: Affirmations help you get out of your own way. They support your dreams in becoming reality.

Every one of us alone has the power to direct the course of our lives by choosing what actions we will or won't take. While sometimes it's easier to believe you don't have a choice, the reality is that you always have a choice to behave and think differently.

FRANCINE WARD

☐

KNOWING YOUR PRIORITIES

As Francine Ward so elegantly points out, the direction that your life takes is the result of choices. As your divine purpose is revealed, it's very important to make these "green choices" deliberate. You must have a strong sense of priorities. What are the places in your life where you are saying yes and you should be saying no? What are the places where you are saying no and you should be saying yes? When you don't make a commitment to being clear about your priorities, it's easy to get all mixed up.

Every day, people come to me and express a sense of being overwhelmed by all that's happening in their lives. The good news is that everyone can grow by *taking charge* of their lives. In my life, the tool I use to keep my priorities straight is a personal digital assistant (PDA). Each day, I can look at my PDA and see what I am to do, and where I can best be of service. Then I am flexible if other priorities come up. I don't make it the law. But it certainly helps guide my life.

I recommend you have a day planner, calendar, or PDA to help you create a path for your daily life. In order to make a difference in your life and the lives of others, you have to be on a path, and then be willing to step off of it when it's appropriate. You want to keep your eyes focused and your mind clear. At the end of this chapter, you'll find morning questions that will further help you get a handle on your daily priorities.

> The key is not to prioritize what's on your schedule, but to schedule your priorities.
> STEPHEN R. COVEY

☐

LETTING GO OF WHAT ISN'T WORKING

Years ago when we had the Tara's Angels store, we had an employee who was not working out. I knew that we were going to have to let her go, but although she was creating problems, I was torn. The caretaker in me wanted to support this woman by letting her stay.

I went to my minister and asked, "How can I let this person go?" She said to me, "What is truly the highest and best for you? In the spiritual realm, that has to be the best for everyone involved." When I thought about it, I realized my minister was right. I could see that firing this employee was the highest and best choice for me, and not just for my ego. Soon after this conversation, I notified the employee, and to my surprise and delight, she was able to find something that was more suitable for her fairly quickly. What a relief that was!

In contrast, what happens when you try to hang onto something that's not working? Can you see that you only keep yourself stuck? And on top of that, you keep everyone else stuck. Hanging on is an easy thing to do—either because you want to be right, want to be good, or want to take care of someone else, as I did with my employee. But what you're actually doing at those times is hanging on for dear life to something that's not serving you.

I think of this wisdom fairly often—*what is truly highest and best for me will be best for everyone involved.* Sometimes it will take a lot of courage to face the truth, but I believe you'll find it's worth the effort in the long run.

> When you cling, life is destroyed; when you hold
> onto anything, you cease to live.
> ANTHONY DE MELLO

□

WORKING THROUGH THE CHALLENGES

Another way you can get stuck on the path of expansion is when you encounter a personal challenge. In your mind, you make a problem bigger than it actually is, and then you can't see a way around it. Instead of dealing with the challenge, you stop on the path and sit in your trouble—feeling terrible and sorry for yourself. There's a saying about this, and it's true—*the best way out is through!*

In dealing with a challenge, ask yourself these questions:

Where does this challenge fit in the scheme of things?

Is it something that needs my immediate attention?

How much of a priority is it?

What is this challenge trying to tell me?

What am I to learn from this?

What are the appropriate steps to be taken?

What is the first step I must take?

When you're in the middle of a challenge, you may need to *push* yourself to see beyond it. But if you back out of it slowly, meditate, and breathe, you can put the challenge outside of yourself and take a good hard look. You can observe the challenge, shifting your perspective from the eyes of challenge to the eyes of possibility. The questions above will help you kick-start this process.

> New ideas stir from every corner. They show up
> disguised innocently as interruptions, contradictions
> and embarrassing dilemmas.
> ROB LEBOW

□

REMAINING FLEXIBLE

Whenever you're tending to something you're growing, it's important to let go of rigidity—the idea that things must unfold in a certain way. This allows your vision to naturally manifest, rather than being forced out in a joyless manner. In my experience, much joy comes from the process of allowing your vision to evolve, through the discoveries you make along your path of growth and evolution. You'll want to balance having a plan with being open to adjusting it when it makes sense to do so.

The need to be flexible reminds me of an experience I had when I began my career as a schoolteacher. In my practice-teaching, I worked with third and sixth graders—but no kindergarteners. After training, my initial real job was as a kindergarten teacher. On the first day, I asked the children to get out their red crayons. This was a long time ago before kids were exposed to accelerated learning from TV and preschool, and half of the children in my class didn't know what the color red was. I remember thinking, *Oh no! Now what?*

Though this shook me at the time, I soon saw that I would have to adjust my teaching plan backward in order to instruct the children about all of the colors. I must have ended up doing something right, because I went on to teach kindergarten for twelve years. Although I enjoyed a twenty-year teaching career, on that first frustrating day, I didn't feel I could ever be a successful teacher. Only by being flexible and remaining open to adjusting to circumstances that came up did I achieve success.

The bend in the road is not the end of the road
unless you refuse to take the turn.
ANONYMOUS

☐

| GROWTH EXERCISE |

Asking the Right Questions to Start the Day

As I manifest a goal, I like having questions to prompt the growth process. Questions allow for more openness for our good to enter. That's why I've already included many questions in this chapter. Below are a set of questions that you can use as part of a morning practice to determine your priorities for the day.

Each morning, sit down with your journal in a relaxing place. Then choose the questions from the list below that resonate the most with you.

- What is the next step for me to take this day in order to move closer to my vision?
- What are the most important things that I need to achieve today?
- What gifts do I have to give today?
- What things might I want to do that could wait for another day?
- Where do I need more courage to activate my vision?
- What new choices do I need to make?
- What do I need to let go of to open myself up to more joy, focus, and energy?
- If I am faced with a challenge or problem, how can I refocus my vision to see the good or the gift inherent in the day's situation?

As in Nature—where you see trees, rose bushes, and grasses evolving and growing with water, soil, and sunshine—growth is available to you too, if you are open to it. You need not stagnate. By consciously living day by day and accepting what feeds your soul and vision, as plants accept their nutrients, you can move your life into the green realm of your dreams.

I am enough of an artist to draw freely upon my imagination.
Imagination is more important than knowledge.
Knowledge is limited.
Imagination encircles the world.

ALBERT EINSTEIN

☐

WHAT'S NEXT?

At times, it's important to break away from all the activity of dream-building and dream maintenance to care for other essential aspects of your life. Your relationships, your body, your spirit, your work—all need care in the same way your dreams do. Chapter 10 encourages you to make breaks and time-outs a regular part of your routine.

I have so much to do today
that I must meditate for two hours
instead of one.
MAHATMA GANDHI

☐

Caring for the Sacred Self

Keep the Kitchen Sink Clean

When we take time for ourselves,
we are cherishing ourselves.
Soon we begin to have a glow about us...
We stop yelling at our children or partners,
and we can give to others from our overflow.
MICHELLE MORRIS SPIEKER

The paradox of our time in history
is that we have taller buildings,
but shorter tempers;
wider freeways, but narrower viewpoints.
We spend more, but have less...
We've conquered outer space, but not inner space.
We've done larger things, but not better things.
DR. BOB MOORHEAD

Up to this point, you've been hard at work growing the magnificence of your life. To keep that magnificent life, you must take care of the vehicle you've been given for traveling through time—*your body.* No one can expect their body to perform well without giving reverence to what it needs and deserves.

In the daily grind, people sometimes get caught up in making money and getting more stuff. With all the emphasis on competition and consumption in our society, it's easy to miss out on what's really important in life, and to neglect your spirit. So for the sake of your body and spirit, the goal of Chapter 10 is to awaken a consciousness within you about how essential it is to take time-outs from the major activities of your days.

> Be mindful of how you approach time.
> Watching the clock is not the same
> as watching the sun rise.
> SOPHIA BEDFORD-PIERCE

□

SCHEDULED SELF-MAINTENANCE

Do you feel important enough to schedule self-care by marking it on your day planner? Would you feel guilty each time, or even some of the time? If you would feel guilty, then you need to be aware of some thought patterns that need to change. These thought patterns will become evident when you start to listen to your self-talk, and they are likely to be the result of influences from society or your family. Self-talk such as *Who do you think you are, taking an afternoon off to get a massage?* could be an echo of a parent's criticism earlier in your life. If you really think it through, you should see that the massage would help you become more productive, present, and content in the big picture.

Author Michelle Spieker points out that while there is a lot of talk about being compassionate with others, less is said about the need to be compassionate with ourselves—about acknowledging our vulnerabilities and needs, as well as our strengths. She recommends having tools to cherish yourself, and remaining true to those tools, especially during the most stressful times. When you have a program of regularly scheduled self-care, you will be less likely to succumb to negative habits that take you off of what Spieker calls "the path of the cherished self." Such negative habits include overworking, not getting enough sleep, eating too much, and spending too much money.

These self-destructive tendencies are all unhealthy ways that we try to take care of ourselves, when we actually should be taking more breaks, getting a good night's sleep, maintaining a healthy diet that keeps us at a desirable weight, and spending within our means. If you do find yourself veering into these undesirable self-soothing patterns, remind yourself to turn instead to the tools of regular self-care, and make extra plans for self-maintenance and repair as necessary.

Since most of us are familiar with all the things people do to keep their cars running smoothly, let's compare a program of scheduled self-care with maintenance of an automobile. Note that some of our self-care will be required daily, whereas other maintenance will be on a weekly, monthly or yearly basis. Whenever it's helpful and practical, I'd like you to insert blocks of time for this self-care into your day planner to help make the plan stick.

Car Maintenance	Essential Self-Maintenance
1. Changing oil.	1. Uplifting your spirit with meditation, self-help classes and inspirational reading that will assure your energy remains steady and reliable...tapping into the tools that will keep your mind on track and soul aloft.
2. Rotating the tires.	2. Altering your routine to spark feelings of aliveness and alertness to safely handle any sudden obstacles.
3. Filling the gas tank.	3. Fueling your body with a delicious, nutritious diet.
4. Getting the car washed and waxed.	4. Pampering yourself with a massage or manicure and then dressing up for a special occasion.
5. Taking care of automobile repairs.	5. Tending to your physical upkeep health by going to the dentist or chiropractor.
6. Visiting a mechanic for preventive maintenance.	6. Going to see your doctor for a yearly physical.

How spiritual can you feel when you're fatigued and burned out? Routine self-maintenance is a great preventative against lethargy and illness. When you start keeping self-care at the top of your mind when you plan your schedule, you'll soon find you're getting more enjoyment out of living.

Personal Maintenance

All biological systems have feedback loops, or a way of signaling threats to balance and the ability to restore balance. The Earth as a whole is the largest scale example we have of a self-regulating 'organism' which is subject to feedback controls, like global warming. Feedback is often slow to emerge.

Paul Hawken, the author of Blessed Unrest has documented and compiled an extensive list of numerous ecological and social grassroots movements around the world. He states that these quiet revolutions are like the world's immune response to the pending economic disease, political corruption, and ecological degradation that surrounds us. They are small and local revolutions, growing from the ground up in a collective response to devastation. There is not one charismatic leader, but many. These movements are powerful in effectiveness, not in domination.

As we take a stand and lead movements for the health of our environment and our communities, we must take action and focus on the health of our own bodies and minds.

One of my passions is holistic health and nutrition. I learned long ago that if I am not feeling healthy, I am of little use to anyone or anything! I am much more creative, connected, empowered, effective, resourceful and inspired when I feel alive. I choose to listen to my body and what it needs. The main things my body needs are whole and fresh food, clean water, body movement, dance, yoga, surfing, walking, and biking, and adequate sleep and rest. Other things that help my physical health are conscious breathing, honest communication, and meditation.

Suggestions:
- Take care of ourselves by eliminating toxins in our bodies
- Eat food that is organic & locally grown
- Eat whole foods that have not been processed
- Minimize sweets & stimulants, and instead try teas & organic fruits
- Use household & bath products that are non-toxic
- Get fresh air and sunshine every day

- Move your body & bring your full awareness into every cell
- Good night sleep
- Superfoods
- Quality – we get what we pay for
- Take deep breaths whenever you remember

Resources:
Paul Hawken: blessedunrest.com
Body Ecology: www.bodyecology.com
Green Made Easy:

Keeping your body healthy
is an expression of gratitude
to the whole cosmos—
the trees, the clouds, everything.
THICH NHAT HANH

□

MESSAGES FROM SPIRIT

Deanna and I took a spiritual journey to India with a wonderful group of Sai Maa Lakshmi Devi's students. We traveled through India, starting in New Delhi, journeying through Varanasi and ending in Puttaparti at Sai Baba's ashram. I found India to be hard travel, although I loved my fellow travelers and their consciousness of love and support.

Mid-journey Deanna took a side trip on her own to make a visit to an organic chocolate farm. I am always amazed and impressed with Deanna's sense of adventure and her courageous ability to journey out into the unknown being guided by Spirit and protected by the angels. I dreamed that she met Willy Wonka in a turban and the next day I continued with the group to visit the ashram at Puttaparti.

Ashram life was a different experience for me. The rooms were not comfortable or inviting. Sitting on marble floors for five hours at a time in silence was hard on me — especially for my behind, and my neck which was injured years ago. During one such silent time I felt a migraine headache coming on and had to leave the meditation hall in a hurry. I got to my room just in time. Because Deanna hadn't arrived yet, I was rooming alone. I was very sick, had no water in my room and couldn't stand up. I felt alone and afraid. No one would know to look after me. What was I going to do?

A few minutes later there was a knock at the door. I struggled to the door to find my wonderful daughter. She took one look at me and said, "Mom, I knew you were sick. I got the 'call' and I came as soon as I could." The "call" is the spiritual connection we have with those we love deeply. She knew she was needed. She stayed with me and nursed me back to health. Sometimes love heals us more than anything else.

> For fast-acting relief,
> try slowing down.
> LILY TOMLIN

□

LIFE OUT OF BALANCE?

Most of us think of the brain as our source of intelligence. However, there is intelligence in every cell of our bodies. When the balance of your life is out of whack and you need a break, your body will let you know. You may feel like you're catching a cold, or just have a sense of being off kilter. Pay attention to these messages from your body, but know that the type of break that you need won't always be the same.

Sometimes when you take a break, you need to take care of your body. However, other times, it may be your spirit, your creativity, or your relationships that need attention. Sometimes we must go into meditation in order to get clear about what's being neglected. When you meditate at a time like this, consider the question:

**What needs attention right now
in order to give my life balance?**

| GROWTH EXERCISE |

Balancing Your Life

When I think about balancing my life, I find it helpful to look at six basic areas. They are:

- Work / Career
- Body
- Spirit
- Relationships
- Creativity
- Fun / Play

Here's an easy way to chart this out:

1. Draw a large circle on a sheet of paper in pencil—this represents your life.
2. Slice it into six pieces, like a pie.
3. Label each of the six slices of your life with one of the categories from the above list.

4. Using a colorful felt-tip pen, mark the paper with a dot for each aspect of your life. If you feel fulfilled in that part of your life, put the dot representing it along the outer edge of the circle by that slice. But if you feel that aspect needs attention, place the dot somewhere within the slice. You'll want to put the dot closer to the center of the circle if you need to devote a lot more attention to it, or more toward the outer edge of that slice if it just needs a little more attention. You get the idea.

5. Now connect all of the dots with your felt-tip pen.

I love this exercise because it gives us a visual image of how we're doing regarding the issue of balance. When your life is perfectly in balance, your wheel of life will be smooth and round—a wheel that rolls along easily. However, when it's out of balance, there will be chunks missing that will make your life more bumpy and difficult.

How did you do? Do you see where you need to focus more energy to achieve a greater life balance?

Let's look more closely at these six areas.

WORK / CAREER

For many people, work/career is an area that gets more than its share of their precious time. Because of the precarious economic period we're in, people feel more pressure to put extra effort into their jobs. In addition, some of us have careers that are more demanding than others. Plus there are long-held societal beliefs that reinforce the work focus, such as "It's hard to make a living."

If work is taking too big of a chunk out of your life, you'll need to look at the beliefs that have kept you glued to your desk. Consider how your own choices and perspectives may be preventing you from making more time for other aspects of living.

For some people, work/career may actually be an area that needs more of their focus. Maybe your job is unsatisfying and draining, or it pays you so little that you're always feeling financial pressure. Is it time for you to begin taking steps toward improving your work situation? The principles, strategies, and exercises throughout this book can help guide you as you go about making changes to support improvement.

> Sometimes it's important to work for that pot of gold.
> But other times it's essential to take time off and to make sure
> your most important decision in the day simply consists of
> choosing which color to slide down on the rainbow.
>
> DOUGLAS PAGELS

□

BODY

In caring for your body, it is imperative that you release the residue of past impressions that get stored in your cells and tissues. Ways to do this include:

- Massage therapy
- Soaking in a hot Epsom salts or mineral bath
- A regular meditation or breath-work practice
- Walking in nature, such as along the beach, in the desert, or in the woods
- A relaxing vacation

Part of this work deals with releasing old emotional pain and wounds that are still held in your body. If you don't know how to work with your difficult feelings, they might get pushed down into your body—letting you think you're moving on. Instead, you're just stuffing your feelings and not healing. The good news is that by traveling the path of forgiveness and understanding, you can work through this kind of pain and let it go.

Often, emotional hurts come when you think people should treat you in a certain way, or that they should act in a particular way. When your expectations are not met, the ego can be very unforgiving. But you can choose to forgive and realize that you're not here to change others. When you embrace this idea, you can reclaim your freedom and set other people free. You can clear your mind, spirit, and body of the clutter of issues of the past.

It's when you recognize what you've been holding onto that you can then heal it with forgiveness. *Recognition* is part of the process of healing. And once you've healed and forgiven, you can move on and do the work that you're supposed to be doing.

When doing forgiveness work, say:

> *I need to know what this is*
> *so that I can be aware of my lack of forgiveness,*
> *and whatever stuck feelings are there,*
> *so I can let it all go.*

and

> *Right now I choose to let go of the pain*
> *associated with this situation.*

Remember This: Seeing your pain from a different perspective and forgiving others is a powerful tool for healing. When you do it, you will feel a sense of release. Nothing can hold you back any longer.

SPIRIT

Dr. Bob Moorhead's quote at the beginning of this chapter is part of his essay, "The Paradox of Our Age." Another insightful line from this piece is, "We've added years to life, but not life to years." What a relevant observation this is. What would it take to add life to your years? What is really important to you? What feeds your soul?

Despite the significance of Spirit, people often comment to me that they don't have twenty minutes a day for a spiritual practice such as meditation or quiet contemplation. What they don't realize is that you can get much more accomplished when you're not stressed, after you've taken the time to plug into the source of unlimited energy, creativity, and consciousness. These short time-outs—for meditating and quiet time alone—are just two of the many ways you can nourish your hungry soul.

Meditation and quiet contemplation can also put you in touch with your purpose—one of the strongest spirit enhancers. To get closer to your purpose, use these sessions to have conversations with your inner self and with God. During the conversations, it's important that you ask the right questions. For instance, if you're going through a stressful period, the wrong question to ask is: *Oh God, why is this happening to me?* "Why" questions are often unproductive because, in our limited view, we usually can't see the bigger intention of the Universe. So instead ask: *What do I need to let go of to be on purpose? What do I need more of in my life?*

Carve out your twenty minutes a day, at least. A routine spiritual practice will keep you moving toward a fuller realization of your Divine potential—like an apple seed growing into a fruit tree. For just as nature's seeds need the right conditions to take root and grow, your spiritual potential also needs the right care. This care requires unhurried time. To make the time, intentionally unplug from the incessant demands and distractions of your plugged-in world on a routine basis.

RELATIONSHIPS

Sometimes we neglect our relationships and then wonder why we're not getting what we want from them. If you feel a lack of connection, or want a greater depth in your relationships, consider putting additional energy into them rather than devoting more time to work or your other regular commitments. Take a break and do something nice for someone else.

You can't give to others without getting something in return — it's a two-way street — and there are different degrees of giving that benefit everyone. For instance, you may give in a broad way on a continual basis, by volunteering for a cause that makes a difference in the world. Or you may make a small or large time commitment — like a day spent accompanying a loved one to a critical doctor's appointment, or a weekend devoted to helping a friend move.

Other times, it could simply be calling someone who is troubled and spending an hour on the phone strategizing solutions to their problem, or sitting down and joking with a loved one who needs a lift. In addition, on a daily basis, you can also give in smaller — but still important — ways, by smiling at a stranger, hugging someone, being patient with an individual who is elderly or physically challenged, or sending a thoughtful thank-you note.

You'll find more ideas about relationships in the final chapter — "Living in Sustainable Joy."

There is more to life
than increasing its speed.
MAHATMA GANDHI

☐

CREATIVITY

Are you overlooking, or missing outlets for, your creative expression? I've found a lot of inspiration for this in Julia Cameron's insightful book, *The Artist's Way: A Spiritual Path to Higher Creativity.* One of her suggestions is to make an artist's date with yourself at least once a week. On this date, you might take a watercolor class, attend a weekly writing-support group, or sing as a member of a choir with regular rehearsals. Breaks for creativity refresh our spirit.

Cameron also recommends producing at least two to three pages of writing every single morning (in addition to journaling). These morning pages can serve as a way to clarify your thoughts and strengthen your writing.

Cameron's other works include the humorous *How to Avoid Making Art*, which discusses methods for breaking through creative blocks (such as the dread of failure), and *The Sound of Paper*, which addresses the sometimes difficult work of finding inspiration for your creative endeavors.

I believe you'll feel more alive when you respond to whatever is calling to your creativity. Consciously allow it to blossom. Don't let a creative impulse wither and die on the vine by ignoring or repressing it.

FUN / PLAY

When was the last time you had fun for the sake of fun? Is this a slice of your pie of life where the dot is closer to the center of the circle than you might like? Fun activities often have no more purpose than to be enjoyable and to lighten your heart.

How do people play? Here are some opportunities:

- Fly a kite by the ocean or a lake or at a neighborhood park.
- Go roller-skating or ice-skating.
- Build a snowman or a sand castle.
- Enjoy board games with friends or family.
- Play baseball, tennis, golf, or croquet.
- Play with a dog, cat, or other pets.
- See a comedy act or a funny film.

How can you blend more fun into your experience of life? As you think about the possibilities, consider how you would feel at the end of each activity. Is it something that *sounds* like fun, but might actually leave you more depleted (like visiting Yosemite at the height of the tourist season and dealing with traffic, congestion and crowds)? Consider whether it's something that you *really* want to do. To one person, a night of dancing with a partner and friends might fit the bill for fun, while someone else might find the music too loud and staying out late too exhausting. You don't want to end up feeling "funned out."

I love to spend time with my family. While Deanna and I love to take exotic journeys, Kirk and I like tropical vacations. Taking a yearly vacation to Kauai with Kirk is one of my great joys. When we are there we swim, snorkel, hike, eat great food, do puzzles, play cards and watch old movies. It is a time of pure relaxation and rejuvenation for me. I find when we return home I have the inspiration and motivation I need to continue my soul's work and my purpose. When we need a break and can't get to Kauai, we pour ourselves a mai tai, sit in the spa, and look at the stars. We're almost there.

Isn't it time you let yourself out to play?
What sort of play is right for you?

Here's an inspirational prayer for getting in touch with the inner knowing that will guide you to more balance and a higher level of self-care.

PRAYER FOR AWARENESS

Deep at the core of my being there is an infinite knower, a know-ingness that is aware of all that I need to live a balanced, fulfilled, and nourished life. I quiet my mind and allow my whole self to listen to this innate wisdom. This wisdom flows to the surface of my being and reveals to me what I need to know.

Where in my life am I out of balance—physically, emotionally, mentally, creatively, and spiritually? What is it that I need to do to bring myself to balance? Is there any area of incompleteness that is draining my energy? What do I need to do to stop this energy drain—complete a project, follow up on a situation, return something I have borrowed, speak my truth, take time to nurture myself?

I make the decision right now to do whatever I need to do to bring peace, balance, and clarity to my life. I know I have everything I need right now to bring balance and harmony into my life. I have all the time, talent, and treasure I need because I live in an infinite and abundant universe. This moment is all there is and I choose to use it wisely. I deserve to live a happy and abundant life and choose to accept that right now. I love and approve of myself the way I am. I allow this love to fill me and guide me to the perfect choices to be in the flow of infinite Good.

Chronos is the world's time...
Kairos is Spirit's time...
We exist in chronos. We long for kairos...
It only takes a moment
to cross from chronos into kairos,
but it does take a moment.
SARAH BAN BREATHNACH

☐

WHAT'S NEXT?

Once you have cultivated your beautiful garden of joyful dreams,
you don't stop growing. In the next chapter, you'll explore how to
continue living a life of infinite possibility and learn how to share
with others from your overflow.

God is delighted to watch our souls enlarge.
MEISTER ECKHART

☐

CHAPTER 11

Living in Sustainable Joy

Be the Change and Spread the Movement by Example

How we spend our days is,
of course, how we spend our lives.
ANNIE DILLARD

Blessed is the season
which engages the whole world
in a conspiracy of love.
HAMILTON WRIGHT MABIE

This journey of learning to live your best life is, in part, a process of learning to love yourself enough to let in the light which is the love, the voice and the healing power of God, as opposed to living in fear and clinging to things and circumstances that do not serve your highest good, that are not green by nature. With faith, you have moved from fear to self-love, to a plane where you are open to receiving all the good that the Universe can deliver. Your openness has allowed good to flow to you, and you are now consciously building the life garden of your dreams. When you manifest your dreams—when you allow your highest good to flow into your life—there is an extra sparkle in your eyes, an added liveliness to your stride, and a contagious joy in your way of living.

In this final chapter, we look at ways you can reach out to others once you have manifested your dreams. And finally, we address how you can handle setbacks in addition to your ongoing growth and expansion.

UPLIFTING YOURSELF INSPIRES OTHERS

When you move up to a new level in your life, you create the space for others around you to do the same. They see that you have continued to move forward with faith and a hearty spirit. They come to know that creating new possibilities in life is an achievable goal. They begin to see the glimmer of sparkling new possibilities in their own lives.

I am part of a weekly discussion group of progressive thinkers and speakers that meets Wednesday mornings. One of our group's regular practices is called "Wins and Acknowledgements." This ritual provides a forum for us to share our recent accomplishments. During this time, we honor the good that has been happening in our lives.

I've shared the progress I've made writing this book. The group has been very excited that my book is becoming a reality. Their excitement is helping me celebrate this manifestation of one of my most important dreams. In turn, my achievement is fertilizing their dreams to write their own books or tackle other challenging projects.

Society doesn't train us to share our accomplishments freely. We are made to feel that doing so is boastful, that it is shameless bragging. But when you share achievements with an open heart to people who care about you, it can feel good for everyone. Positive energy pulls everyone forward.

| GROWTH EXERCISE |

Sharing the Dream

Who might be inspired by hearing about the manifestation of your dream? Who would want to celebrate this achievement with you? Make some phone calls or lunch dates to share your progress with those who would draw strength from your positive efforts and be moved to authentically celebrate your progress. It's your right to take pride in all that you've accomplished.

WORKING TOGETHER IN COMMUNITY:
HOW I LEARNED TO ASK FOR HELP

Maintaining your dream is not something you need to do alone. While the major part of the responsibility rests on your shoulders, there are many ways others can offer support. When we get our friends involved, we can continue to build our dream much larger than we could construct it by ourselves. Certainly this has been true for us with the creation of our spiritual center, and it's there that I learned an interesting lesson about getting help.

Once our spiritual center became a reality, I realized I needed support from volunteers—people to help set up our space for services, a hospitality chairperson to organize the greeting of congregants, people to serve as guest ambassadors, and more. At first I thought it would be enough to make general announcements at our Sunday services and place requests for volunteers in our weekly bulletin; but these approaches didn't pull in the number of people that we needed. Everyone is so busy. It was easy for congregants to rationalize not getting involved by figuring that someone else would jump in. I eventually discovered that many people needed to be asked by Kirk or me directly if they'd be willing to pitch in and help.

I've noticed that making a personal request really makes a huge difference in getting results. When we make a direct request of others, we honor them. We acknowledge their ability to make a valuable contribution. People like the feeling that what they have to offer is truly worthwhile.

From time to time, I forget the lesson of how important individual requests can be, and I fall back into making general pitches for volunteers. Then I remember that I need to ask people personally for help. Like many other lessons in life, this is one I need to relearn periodically.

Manifestation

I love working with plants, from the farm or garden to the kitchen. My life's work is to care for the earth and its people. When I was first learning about permaculture, one of my teachers called our practice of working with the earth practical mysticism. We're plugging back into the earth, and doing something to create change and an abundance of solutions. This was to me naturally spiritual – I am using nature's lessons to live in the world. The journey for me has been about personal growth and practical service. I am so much more effective when I am in the flow of creativity, peace and openness.

How can we work on our inner ecology & outer environment at the same time? In my opinion, this growth and service is needed now more than ever. Fast. Now. Recently I had a series of deep realizations, and my personal mission statement became clear to me. My personal mantra: I cultivate personal growth & healing every single day, so that I am able to affect greater change outside myself for the benefit of all beings in all places for all time.

Sometimes I spiral in and out of presence and patience and fear and overwhelm. I always come back to my mission, and remember that solutions exist. I need to be as available and open as possible to receive them, and then give them back in a new way.

Ways to manifest our inner ecology with our outer environment:

- Observe ourselves and the world without judgement
- Go Deep
- Take note and take Action
- Look for solutions
- Transform overwhelm into inspiration
- Grow peace
- Take compassion based actions that integrate soul and the earth
- Have fun, or change the plan!

So while you're enjoying the manifestation of your dream, don't forget to get others involved so you can create something even larger with their support. Remind yourself occasionally to reach out to people in this way. Learning to ask for help may feel humbling at times, but it is also empowering.

Before you ask someone for assistance, give thought to who best matches a particular task. Then, after considering people's skill sets, look at why individuals give of their time, including the idea of making a worthwhile contribution. Other basic reasons for contributing assistance include having a fresh opportunity to work with others, the satisfaction of helping someone, experiencing the enjoyment of the activity, and developing new skills, knowledge, and contacts. Think about how many of these gains you can provide to the people you might call upon for support.

Another part of asking for help is acknowledging those who make the effort to become part of your team. Once someone makes headway on your behalf, tell them directly how pleased you are with whatever they have accomplished. Look for ways to reciprocate by being there to support their goals. When it's appropriate, make their contributions known to others. In addition, find ways to make their contribution of time fun, including celebrating your progress occasionally with a special lunch or other event.

While maintaining your dream life doesn't have to be a one-person job, asking for help might require developing a new perspective. Many of us have been indoctrinated into thinking that we need to get everything done independently. You may feel that asking for support is a sign of weakness—of not being up on your game. On the contrary, honoring your needs enables you to be there on a more productive level for yourself and for others. If you didn't make the mental shift to allow yourself to ask for support while reading Chapter 8 ("Communicating Your Plans"), then do it now. For more ideas on "asking," revisit Chapter 8.

GROWTH EXERCISE
Meditation for Support

Get into your quiet space, and take a few moments to relax your body. Make adjustments where needed to work out any areas of tightness, such as by gently rolling your neck, rubbing your temples with your fingertips, or stretching your lower back. Then breathe in a relaxed manner, and begin to think of the bounty that is currently your life. Feel appreciation for all that the Universe has brought to you on your path. Once you fill yourself up with feelings of appreciation, meditate on the following questions:

Where in my life would support be most beneficial?

What type of person would best fit each role?

Who might be willing to support me in this way?

If I do not know such a person, how can I find someone?

For each need, visualize talking with a person and successfully asking for help. Think of the words that you would use. Think of the request that you would make. See this person fulfilling this need in a satisfactory way. See yourself showering this person with appreciation and love. See both of you benefiting from this exchange.

Revisit this meditation as often as you need to in order to work through the areas where support would be helpful. Come back to this series of meditations at a later date when you are once again feeling in need of greater support in your life.

By focusing on fulfillment with this mental imagery, you are shifting energy to the vibrations which would be present if all of your needs were met. This adjustment brings forth more support from the Universe. Your imagination creates new possibilities for fulfillment and joy.

> You create your opportunities
> by asking for them.
> SHAKTI GAWAIN

□

ACTIVELY LOVING OTHERS

When your dream life has come into existence, you are in a better position than ever to open up your heart and share your love with other people. So in addition to seeing what support you need at this point, think about how you can share your love with others.

How can you give from your own overflow? A basic question I like to ask is *What would love do now?* This intention to be loving is what brings us joy.

An important way to be loving starts with recognizing that there is beauty in everyone, even if that beauty is still waiting to be expressed. Holding this thought, look around your world and see how you might create the space for other people to grow into their own greatness. Sometimes all it takes for someone is the belief of one other supportive person. How could you view at least one other person differently? On this note, consider the following story.

STORY: *THE AGING MONKS GET NEW EYES*

Beside a magnificent forest in Germany, centuries ago, half a dozen monks in their sixties and seventies ran an ancient monastery. Their leader, an abbot, was gravely concerned about the future of the monastery and their order, as well as who would care for the monks as they continued to grow older. While the monastery offered Sunday services, the congregation had dwindled down from sixty people to only two or three beyond the men who lived there.

One sunny morning, the abbot roamed alone in the woods, contemplating the problem of how to make a better future for those at the monastery. Seeing no solution, he tried to lift his spirits by listening to the concert of birdsongs being performed around him. Just then, down the path rode the mayor of the nearest village on horseback. An old friend of the abbot, the mayor paused on his journey to talk with him.

The abbot poured out his worries to the mayor, and asked if his friend could think of what would be best to do. Considering the situation, the mayor admitted his villagers had stopped going to the monastery because Sunday services had become dry and boring. Then he added, "But I can tell you that the villagers and I have long suspected that someone at the monastery is the Messiah."

That night, the abbot and his five fellow monks gathered at the long oak table in the monastery dining hall for supper. The abbot shared his experience of encountering the mayor in the forest and disclosed what the politician had said about what he and the villagers believed. The assembled monks looked around at one another with wide eyes.

After that evening, the six men at the monastery began to see each other differently, and they started to be kinder with each other, more supportive, and more patient. Soon their vibrancy grew, and this began to be reflected in the Sunday services they offered at the monastery chapel. More and more of the mayor's villagers began to attend the services once more, and word spread to other villages near the forest. People from additional towns journeyed to the services too. With time, younger men joined the order. After several years, the monastery was thriving as it had been in years past.

This story of the aging monks reveals the power of recognizing the best in everyone, instead of what doesn't feel good. When that change of perspective is focused on one person, it can change a life. Could you be the person in someone else's life that makes all the difference? Who could you help move away from insecurity and fear, steering them instead toward their fulfillment and joy? Live your life knowing that we are all here to love and be loved.

The real voyage of discovery
consists not in seeking new landscapes
but in having new eyes.
MARCEL PROUST

□

GROWING PAST DORMANT SEASONS

Despite all you've accomplished, there will still be occasional fallow times ahead, for they are part of the process of life. When you pass through these quieter phases, know that there is always good to be found. Seeing the good in the more challenging periods is part of having a glass half full rather than a glass half empty mentality.

For instance, less busy and less demanding seasons are opportunities to rethink your life garden's modus operandi and reconsider your choice of "crops" and your priorities for future "plantings." During dormant periods, you'll want to go inward for understanding and direction. This is when you need to take more time for quiet contemplation.

> When it is dark enough,
> you can see the stars.
> RALPH WALDO EMERSON

□

In the fallow season, it's also helpful to turn to trusted people who will remind you that there is plenty of potential lying beneath the surface of your life. To those who know that though your life garden may have less apparent growth above the ground, there are plenty of seeds of possibilities for you to cultivate. When you need encouragement because of a dormant phase, allow yourself to be vulnerable and open to someone else pulling you up to a more enlightened perspective.

It's natural for everyone to face transitions and less busy periods. What you must do is keep having more beginnings than endings. At these transition points in life, find inspiration for your re-visioning work in the saying, "What the caterpillar calls the end of life, the master calls the butterfly."

The ability to create new beginnings also comes from staying in the movement of life, rather than getting stuck in a fallow period. During the dormant times, use the mantras, "This too shall pass" and "Spirit's grace is my sufficiency." While you are seeking the good during the fallow phase, also continue to move forward with incessant additional improvements to your life's garden. Don't be afraid to reinvent yourself. Keep going and keep growing.

> Come forth into the light of things.
> Let nature be your teacher.
> WILLIAM WORDSWORTH

☐

THE CIRCLE OF LIFE

Life is cyclical, and over the years, you will witness your life's garden growing through its phases. As you plan, plant, tend, harvest, and then plant once more, you can move time and again through the basic processes in this book. Nature likes round things. In a sense, there are really no beginnings and endings in a joyful life — it's all one long journey of growth. This book can be a tool that you use throughout your life.

Because you have worked through this book to these final pages, you are undoubtedly a person dedicated to your ongoing growth and personal expansion. I'm sure you have many ideas for how you want to keep growing. But for those times when you need some inspiration, try the following meditation.

| GROWTH EXERCISE |

The Continual Growth Meditation

Prepare yourself to meditate. Close your eyes, and see yourself sitting on a bench in your garden of possibilities. Feel yourself relaxing, and once you're comfortable, look about at your surroundings through your mind's eye. After taking a moment or two to appreciate the beauty of your garden, ask yourself the following questions:

What do I still need to learn about my garden of life?

What is left for me to do here?

What is my life garden trying to tell me about how I still need to grow?

What choice could I make right now about my garden of life that would generate more life and energy?

Asking questions is a springboard for growth that I have used repeatedly throughout this book. Questioning is a great way to conjure up original thought and new insights. Continue to ask yourself questions, choosing ones that are true to what you need to be seeking. If you discover that your questions are keeping you stuck, ask yourself new questions to fulfill your commitment to being green— a way of living your very best life that allows your highest self and goodness to be revealed.

The great Walter Russell, a painter-sculptor-architect-scientist in the early twentieth century, is profiled in a wonderful little book by Glenn Russell titled *The Man Who Tapped the Secrets of the Universe*. Russell believed that anyone who could find an inner joy in self-discovery could also experience something greater than success. Glenn Clark quoted Russell in his book:

The successful man is one who is considered to have made a success of his life according to modern standards which include the accumulation of money, properties and an honorable place in the world for notable achievement and financial worth. In other words, the successful man is generally conceived as being one who accumulates values which can be rated by Bradstreet's. But there is something still greater than all of that; there is the Life Triumphant which transcends all material success. The Life Triumphant is that which places what a man gives to the world in creative expression far ahead of that which he takes from it of the creations of others. And it should be every man's greatest ambition to be that kind of man. With that desire in the heart of every man there could be no greed or selfish unbalance, nor could there be exploitation of other men, or hatreds, or wars or fears of wars.

Remember This: When you live your best life, you stay in a perpetual state of curiosity and wonder. You triumph because you're always learning. You continue to gain a greater understanding of yourself and others. You are not a static being, but a human being ever stretching to new levels, cultivating an evergreen life.

Green Intention Affirmation:
I am filled with inspiration, vision, and wonder.
I reach for ever-increasing joy.

WHAT'S NEXT?

There is a famous quote by Karen Kaiser Clark that is short and to the point, yet it speaks volumes: "Life is change. Growth is optional. Choose wisely."

We are presented with opportunities to "choose wisely" everyday whether we know it or not. Most of the time our habits or instincts choose for us and we never realize an opportunity to grow is at hand. After reading this book and completing the exercises, Deanna and I hope every choice from now on is a wise one.

What are you willing to do now? Who are you willing to become? Always be open to cultivating new levels of fulfillment in your life. Embrace and enjoy your many blessings. Living your best life with a green intention radiates many more blessings. Go in courage. Go in love. Go with questions. Go with wings . . . . Go green.

We cannot live a choiceless life.
We are either choosing to stretch our minds...
setting new goals, seeking to expand our boundaries...or
we are choosing to be victims of the events,
circumstances, and people in our lives.
ERNEST HOLMES

☐

We shall not cease from exploration,
and the end of all our exploring will be
to arrive where we started
and know the place
for the first time.

T. S. ELIOT

About the Authors

Rev. Sandy Moore graduated from USC with a degree in teaching and subsequently earned a Masters in Educational Administration followed by 20 years in public service as a school teacher.

In 1980, Sandy and her husband Kirk found spiritual comfort in New Thought and became involved with the Redondo Beach Church of Religious Science. Years later, they both completed ministerial training and now devote their careers to Religious Science and are currently the spiritual and music directors of Mission Viejo Center for Spiritual Living in California. The Center is actively involved in bringing world-renowned authors, lecturers and speakers to Orange County as well as providing numerous outreach activities, including ministries devoted to the environment, health, and peace.

Sandy and Kirk opened Tara's Angels in San Juan Capistrano in 1992 as a way of honoring their daughter who died tragically in an auto accident. The specialty shop and their story gained national attention with a cover story in People Magazine and an in-depth piece on the TV news magazine Dateline. Sandy started facilitating a regular support group at the store, and Kirk wrote an account of their spiritual odyssey in the book *Tara's Angels: One Family's Journey of Courage and Healing* and its sequel *Touched by Tara – The Healing Power of Love*.

Deanna Moore is a chef, educator, designer and artist who lives and teaches the art and science of ecologically sustainable living. She has taught in elementary schools, colleges, at festivals and community centers throughout the country on topics of biodiesel, sustainable food, gardening, tree planting, permaculture design and eco-spirituality. Deanna holds a Master's Degree in Ecologically Sustainable Education from Prescott College and a B.A. in Culture, Ecology, and Sustainable Community from New College of California. Deanna has worked with indigenous cultures in Africa, India and Canada, exchanging seeds, inspiration and promoting the value of traditional knowledge in an ecologically sustainable culture. Currently she lives in Southern California where she provides green design and consultation services for Green Insight Designs, and owns FLOW Foods, a sustainable food business.